What People Have Sa

"Dr. Tim Adams addresses a ... relevant than people realize in his book, *What the Bible Really Says About Drinking Alcohol*. His research from the perspectives of science, medicine, and Scripture all point the reader to a fuller understanding of God's Word and alcoholic beverages. The book flows logically from one topic to another. This book is a must for Christ-followers."

Dr. Kevin Shearer, Pastor, Hattiesburg, MS

"In tell it like it is fashion, Dr. Adams addresses the Scriptural truth about drinking alcohol. His captivating writing both expounds and clarifies God's word in a way that is meaningful and relevant to today's Christians. If you want to understand what God really says about alcohol, read this book!"

Melissa Beaty, High School Mathematics Teacher

"I have always believed the Bible is clear about drinking alcohol. My problem was not being able to adequately defend that belief. What Dr. Adams has done in *What the Bible Really Says about Drinking Alcohol* is give us a resource to do just that. It is an easy read and to the point. Every Christ Follower should want to be able to share what 'God really says about alcohol'. This book will help us all in doing just that."

Nelson Wilson, Dentist, Old Hickory, TN

What the Bible Really Says About Drinking Alcohol

by

Dr. Tim Adams

What the Bible Really Says
About Drinking Alcohol

Copyright © 2018 by Dr. Tim Adams
All rights reserved.
ISBN-13: 978-1722030834
ISBN-10: 1722030836

No part of this book may be reproduced in any form without permission in writing from the author.

All scripture quotations are from the King James Version of the Bible unless otherwise stated.

Printed in the United States of America by Shepherd's Voice Ministries.

Cover Design: Tim Adams and Eric Beaty
Editor: Melissa Beaty

Contents

Preface
Acknowledgments

Chapter One
When Wine is Not Really Wine!
1

Chapter Two
When Noah and Lot Got Drunk
9

Chapter Three
Condemned By Example
17

Chapter Four
The Rechabites and the Nazarites
21

Chapter Five
Solomon on Booze
29

Chapter Six
Nothing Hidden, Nothing Excused
37

Chapter Seven
Kings and Priests
45

Chapter Eight
Did Jesus Really Serve Alcohol?
51

Chapter Nine
"Not Given to Much Wine"
65

Chapter Ten
The Double Portrait of Wine
71

Chapter Eleven
Is Unfermented Wine in Bible Days a Myth?
75

Chapter Twelve
Who Knows What Constitutes Drunkenness?
83

Chapter Thirteen
Three Biblical Motives for Total Abstinence
89

Chapter Fourteen
Timothy's Medicine Cabinet
97

Chapter Fifteen
What Was Served In The Upper Room?
103

Chapter Sixteen
Troublesome Passages
107

Chapter Seventeen
Reviewing the Discovery
127

Chapter Eighteen
How Can I Stop Drinking Alcohol?
135

Chapter Nineteen
Alcohol and the Devil
141

Chapter Twenty
Wishing for an Alcohol-Free World
159

Bibliography
163

Preface

More than twenty-seven centuries ago in a land called Judah, a prophet named Isaiah cried, "None calleth for justice, nor any pleadeth for truth: they trust in vanity, and speak lies; they conceive mischief, and bring forth iniquity....**truth is fallen in the street**." (See Isaiah 59:4,14)

I have been a pastor for thirty-seven years. Twenty five of those years I've literally watched the truth about drinking alcohol fall in the streets to be twisted and trampled. Some doctors say it is good for your health. Drinkers say a little bit can't hurt you. In the present age, preachers, for the most part, don't say anything about it from their God-given pulpits. I have only one concern - what does God say about it?

I have no pet peeves about alcohol. I've never been abused by an alcoholic. My parents were Christians who believed in total abstinence. I have witnessed, in the pastorate, for nearly half a century how alcohol has deceived and destroyed families given to my charge. I have been angry at times, but more brokenhearted for the ravages of alcohol in America. However, the motivation for this book rises higher than sympathy for a problem that is killing a nation. It is an unswerving call to defend God's truth on the subject of alcohol and call the drinker to repentance.

I could write this book from statistical evidence alone condemning alcohol for the catastrophic damage it has done to our world. Likewise, I could take up the debate from a denominational perspective since some denominations give alcohol consumption a shameless green light while others preach teetotalism almost rabidly. Which denomination is right? One verse of Scripture suffices to end the debate. Romans 3:4 says, "let God be true and every man a liar."

You've heard, "What you don't know will not hurt you." I am compelled to tell you this is patently false when it comes to the Word of God. Ignorance of the Word of God can be very costly when it comes to giving an account to God about our behavior. In other words, if we are mistaken about the use of alcoholic beverages because we simply have not studied the entire witness in Scripture on the subject, we will still be held accountable to God.

Whether the family influenced drinking, whether a preacher lied against the Word of God, whether social pressures convinced us that a drink at the company party was acceptable, or even we pridefully believe that drinking alcohol in moderation is not harmful, all that really matters is what God says about this subject. Man's opinion is not the authority. God's Word is the final authority.

Contrary to established opinion the Bible has much to say on drinking alcohol. Faithful and honest examination of the Bible will yield a truthful conclusion. Ignorance of the truth is inexcusable. It is time to resurrect the "truth that has fallen in the streets." What does God REALLY say about drinking alcohol?

Dr. Tim Adams

Acknowledgments

The first honor for this publication should go to God for the constant urge in my spirit to write such a volume and to His vigil over my mind to provide the continual flow of content.

I would like to express a posthumous praise for my parents who both, just three weeks apart in 2017, entered that land where nothing defileth. They exemplified a sober life. They urged me on to Christ for salvation. They raised me to live by the Bible.

I am exceedingly grateful for my wife of more than four decades who has wholeheartedly supported God's call on my life. I have always considered her the perfect pastor's wife. She has never had anything but praise for my preaching, and her smile is continually my anchor in depressing times. I walk in the shadow of her overwhelming goodness.

I am indebted to Melissa Beaty who took time out of her incredibly busy schedule to put the editing of this book on fast track. I have been a writer for 37 years in ministry, but this dear lady has taught me a few things in the discipline.

I am profoundly thankful to Eric Beaty who helped me design the cover for this book. Between my thoughts and his design skill, it turned out pretty good, I think, for the first attempt in this art form.

Last, but certainly not least, I express my Christian love for a brother, confidant, companion in South American missions, and true friend. He was a constant encourager during this writing project. Thank you Dr. Kevin Shearer for the bond we've kept since 1998, and may it turn out for the glory of God.

Chapter One

When Wine is Not Really Wine!

The old adage is quite familiar, "If it looks like an elephant, sounds like an elephant, and smells like an elephant it is probably an elephant." What about the parable of the elephant that originated in India around 500 B.C. in Buddhist texts? The story is quite interesting if you have not heard it. Four blind men were given the task to examine an elephant by touch to see if they could identify the animal. Each man was to touch a certain part of the animal. The first blind man's hands landed on the trunk and he identified the animal as a thick snake. The second blind man's hands touched the elephant's ear and he identified the object as a fan. The third touched the elephant's leg and thought he was touching a pillar post in a building that had been carved to feel like a tree trunk. The last touched the animal's tail and thought he had hold of a rope.

The stated moral of this Buddhistic meandering is that human beings tend to conclude whole truths on partial experiences. The one constant variable in this Indian folklore is that all the men were blind. Many people approach the Bible and its various subjects that way. Regrettably they are blind to the full witness of Scripture on a topic and they begin to justify their beliefs on limited knowledge without a willingness to dig deeper in God's Word. Ultimately they sin and "know not what they are doing."

If you are new to the discussion we must remember that the Bible, our authority for any question in life, was written in two primary and unfamiliar languages to the average American. The Old Testament was written in Hebrew. The New Testament was written in Greek. Having that awareness, it is impossible to make an intelligent conclusion concerning how God feels about drinking alcohol until you examine the Bible in its original languages. You can stop right now and thank God that you do not have to put countless hours into such a study. Many others have done that task already, presenting their findings in understandable terms.

Acts 17:11 describes the Berean Christians as "more noble than those in Thessalonica, in that they received the word with all readiness of mind, and searched the scriptures daily, whether those things were so." I implore you to examine the following conclusions derived through countless hours of Biblical research and join me in adopting a mindset about alcohol that aligns with the Word of God.

To begin our examination of what the Bible says about consuming alcohol, let us lay a foundation in factual truth. In the English translations, the Bible, for the most part, only uses two English words to reference alcoholic beverages: "wine" and "strong drink." The word "whiskey" is not in the Bible. The word "vodka" is not in the Bible. The word "beer" is not in the Bible. The word "alcohol" is not in the Bible. The words we use today to indicate alcoholic drinks are simply not in the Bible, and that fact becomes problematic when people start comparing modern day alcoholic beverages to the beverages in the Bible.

Today's whiskey, if labeled 100 proof, has a 50 percent alcohol content in volume. Vodka typically boasts a 40 percent alcohol content. Beer is the lowest on the totem pole of alcoholic beverages having a 4 to 6 percent alcohol content, although if you want to pay $100 for a 24 ounce bottle of Samuel Adams Utopia, you can get 27 percent alcohol into your bloodstream.[1]

Most conservative Biblical resources point out that today's wine, which sometimes reaches 12-20 percent alcohol content, is nothing like the Biblical wine which had no alcohol content when first squeezed out of the grape and only reached a maximum content of 4 percent after

---

[1] Michelle Bryner, "How Much Alcohol Is In My Drink?" https://www.livescience.com/32735-how-much-alcohol-is-in-my-drink.html.

fermentation was completed. To increase the fermentation and alcoholic content beyond 4 percent, artificial means such as adding yeast are necessary. It is common knowledge that alcohol kills yeast cells which in turn kills the process of fermentation beyond a 10 percent alcohol content. Yeast cells convert the sugar to alcohol, but if there is no more yeast, there is no more fermentation. To reach today's wine alcohol content, winemakers must add sulfur dioxide and Saccharomyces (cultured GMO yeasts) or engage in a distillation process, none of which were even known in Bible days.[2] So, to speak of the "wine and strong drink" in Bible times as if it compared to today's alcoholic beverages is at best comparing apples tod oranges and at worst intellectual dishonesty. The wine and strong drink of Bible times was diluted with water, further reducing the alcohol content. There is no valid comparison.

Another Biblical fact that must be considered, and perhaps the most crucial for ascertaining the truth in this discussion, is to know that basically there are two words in Hebrew for "wine." The first word, used 141 times in the ancient text, is the word *yayin* (pronounced *yah-yen*). Gesenius' Lexicon identifies its root meaning to be "effervescing or bubbling," indicating its intoxicating properties. There is one thing for sure. In the first appearance of this word, Genesis 9:21, the Bible makes it clear that what Noah drank caused him to be "drunken." Of the 141 occasions where *yayin* appears in the Old Testament, I found only two mysterious passages where there would be any question about the word meaning anything other than an intoxicating drink. Most of the passages, when you examine the context, obviously refer to a fermented drink. More will be examined on this in Chapter Sixteen.

In the 13 verses where "wine" and "strong drink" are mentioned together in the same passage the meaning is intoxicating alcoholic drink.[3] We can be sure that when Samson took the Nazarite vow he was not forbidden to

---

[2] Scott J. Shifferd, "What Kind of Wine Did Jesus Drink?" https://godsbreath.net/2011/05/20/did-jesus-drink-wine/

[3] See Numbers 6:3, Deuteronomy 14:6, Judges 13:4, Judges 13:7, 1 Samuel 1:15, Proverbs 20:1, Proverbs 31:6, Isaiah 5:22, Isaiah 28:7, Isaiah 29:9, Isaiah 56:12, Micah 2:11, and Luke 1:15.

drink grape juice. (See Judges 13:7) It was alcoholic wine (*yayin*) that was forbidden. When Abigail, Nabal's wife, brought David and his soldiers two bottles of wine, she brought alcoholic wine because her husband, according to God's word, was a drunkard that died from the effects of alcohol (1 Samuel 25:37). We can also be reasonably sure that Job's sons and daughters were not as "perfect, upright, God-fearing, and hating evil" as their father because they were partying with alcoholic wine in their eldest brother's house when the tornado came and dropped the roof on their heads and killed them. The morning of their deaths, their father, the patriarch Job, as was his custom, was praying for his sons and offering burnt offerings to appease the wrath of God, for in the words of this righteous man, "it may be that my sons have sinned, and cursed God in their hearts." (See Job 1:5) They were sinning and evidently the sin unto death. (See 1 John 5:16) How we need to pray for our family and friends who've given their mouths to the cursed liquid from hell!

Yayin is fermented alcoholic wine according to the most prominent textual evidence. William Edwy Vine, who wrote more than forty-five reference works on Biblical studies, stated in his *Expository Dictionary of OT Words*, "Yayin clearly represents an intoxicating beverage."[4]

In contrast, the other word used in the Old Testament for wine is *Tiyrowsh* (pronounced Tee-rowsh). Again, I have examined the 38 verses in which this word appears and nearly without exception the meaning is a non-alcoholic beverage. How so? Proverbs 3:10 is a self-indicative passage, where no mistake can be made. *Tiyrowsh*, in this passage certainly refers to grape juice. "So shall thy barns be filled with plenty, and thy presses shall burst out with new wine." Even a third grader who is familiar with "wine presses" understands that unfermented wine comes from grapes pressed out till the juice flows. That product has to wait for natural or artificial processes to ferment.

The modern mind knows that you can't get grape juice from wine but you most certainly need grape juice to produce wine. The Biblical mind would be puzzled by our thinking and say, "Of course you've got wine

---

[4] W. E. Vine, "Wine," StudyLight. https://www.studylight.org/dictionaries/vot/w/wine.html.

when you've got grape juice." We have a culture barrier and a time differential of about 2000-4000 years that prevents us from accepting that anything called "wine" could be grape juice. Yet, this is exactly the Bible's distinction: one word for fermented alcoholic wine-*yayin*, and one word for fresh squeezed grape juice also called wine but not alcoholic-*tiyrowsh*. Yet both are called wine in the English translation.

To help us understand that wine can refer to unfermented grape juice, let us examine a passage from Genesis. When Isaac was deceived by Jacob into conveying the firstborn blessing on him instead of Esau, Isaac began the blessing by saying, "Therefore God give thee of the dew of heaven, and the fatness of the earth, and plenty of corn and wine." (Genesis 27:28) Esau was a farmer and a hunter. Isaac's blessing on the wrong boy simply called for God to bless the grain of his field and the grapes of his vineyard. He was in no way speaking of wine in the sense of a fermented beverage. He was simply asking God to provide a bountiful harvest.

God blesses man with grapes but you will never find God producing alcoholic beverages. Man takes what God gives him and corrupts it because of his evil heart. If left alone, grapes will ferment and sour as a result of the curse upon the earth due to man's sin. Yes, if man had never sinned there would not be any alcoholic beverages because alcohol only forms through the corruption and deterioration of grapes. This is artificially hastened through human intervention with the introduction of yeast. Isaiah 65:8 is unquestionably speaking of wine that has no alcohol when he says, "the new wine is found in the cluster." Who would declare themselves so ignorant to claim this reference to wine is something other than grape juice? The simplest mind can deduce Isaiah is referring to the juice of the grape, yet it is called "new wine."

There are three other words occasionally used in the Old Testament to reference "wine." *Aciyc* (pronounced ah-seek) refers to "sweet wine" as in Isaiah 49:26 and Amos 9:13, and was the primary word used to indicate newly squeezed grape juice "the product of the same year."[5] Further study reveals that this *aciyc* (wine) has the capacity for fermentation. Of course it would ferment in a year's time, especially in

---

[5] Vine, "Wine."

that culture, if something wasn't done to prohibit fermentation! Joel 1:5 seems to point out the distinction between *aciyc* and *yayin*, declaring God's destruction of Israel's *aciyc* since they were turning it into alcoholic *yayin*. Therefore *aciyc* is most likely unfermented, sweet grape juice.

The Old Testament also refers to "red wine", *chemer* in Hebrew (pronounced heh-mer). It occurs 7 times and means "to be boiling/foaming," as in fermentation, and "to be red" like the color of blood or the appearance of being inflamed. This word clearly points to intoxicating alcoholic wine as confirmed by Daniel's description of the Babylonian feast in Belshazzar's court (Daniel 5).

One other Hebrew word is used, *shemarim*, and is found in a single reference, Isaiah 25:6. *Shemarim* is "wine on the lees," or wine that has been sitting on the dregs for a long time. *Shemarim* is obviously alcoholic.

We need not go any further in the examination of the Biblical words for "wine" to ask the PARAMOUNT QUESTIONS. Why did God use so many words for wine in the Old Testament if the wine in Bible days is the same alcoholic wine that people drink today in parties, restaurants, and at the table for fancy occasions? Why, in the two most prominent words used in the Old Testament, did God make a clear distinction between grape juice and alcoholic wine? Why didn't He just let everybody who reads the Bible figure that out for themselves based on the context of the passage? I would invite you to stay on board because the answer is forthcoming.

If the Old Testament makes a distinction between wine that is grape juice and wine that is alcoholic, is there anything like that distinction in the New Testament? There is only one primary word used for "wine" in the New Testament, the Greek word *oinos*. It is interesting to know that the person who is drunk with wine was called in Bible days an *oinopotes*, indicating a person who is given to and overpowered by the alcoholic drink. The English word which comes from *oinopotes* is "winebibber." Jesus was accused of being a winebibber but the accusation was false and slanderous. This word *oinos* is almost exclusively referencing alcoholic wine, as evidenced by a simple examination of the context of each appearance. However, there are occasions where *oinos* is definitely unfermented, as in John 2:9-10, Matthew 9:17, and Revelation 6:6.

In Acts 2:13 there is a single mention of a wine that was called *gleukos*, The mocker's conclusion about Pentecost was that the people were "full of new wine (*gleukos*)." Note that this was the judgment of the mockers, not the actual reason for the phenomenon at Pentecost. Yet, we must fairly describe this referenced "new wine" as grape juice of a noted type that could be intoxicating. By its very name, glucose, we ascertain that this wine was laced with saccharine which hastened the fermenting process, a conclusion supported by James Strong.[6] However, Plato, Aristotle, Hippocrates and other ancient writers strongly defend that this *gleukos* was new, sweet wine which was non-intoxicating and safe.[7] Once sweet wine turns alcoholic it is no longer sweet because the yeast has converted the sugar to ethanol. Given the non-intoxicating nature of *gleukos* it is interesting that the mockers paid these Spirit-filled people at Pentecost an unintended compliment. There would be no reason to accuse them of being drunk on *gleukos*, if they were regular drinkers of alcoholic *oinos*. The mocking comment brings out the fact that these disciples of Jesus took seriously the admonitions against drinking in Proverbs and the New Testament.

The most important observation about New Testament references to wine is that not once does any Biblical writer speak of the substance in the cup presented at the Lord's Supper as *oinos*. It is always referred to as "the fruit of the vine." Why that distinction? Biblical writers clearly did not want anyone to believe that Jesus served alcoholic wine. Therefore, any denomination that puts alcoholic wine in their Lord's Supper communion cups have departed from the New Testament and have committed a sacrilege, an egregious wickedness. What have they done to a struggling alcoholic? What have they said to the children of their congregation?

---

[6]James Strong, "Strong's Definitions," Blue Letter Bible. https://www.blueletterbible.org/lang/lexicon/lexicon.cfm?Strongs=G1098&t=KJV&ss=1.

[7]David Brumbelow, *Ancient Wine and the Bible: The Case for Abstinence* (Carrollton: Free Church Press, 2011), 175.

That God would not allow *oinos* to refer to that substance commemorating His blood shed for our sins on the cross brings us back to one of the paramount questions. Why did God make the distinction between wine that was alcoholic and wine that was mere grape juice, that distinction found in both Testaments. As we will see as we examine more passages, God makes the distinction so He can constantly warn against the evils of alcohol consumption. But, will man listen?

Even in the natural realm, men make distinctions to warn against danger. A herpetologist, one who studies amphibians and reptiles, will speak of poisonous and non-poisonous snakes. Descriptions of triangular heads, pits above the nose for sensing prey, oblong slits for eye pupils rather than round pupils all distinguish to some degree the poisonous viper from the non-venomous snake. Isn't it ironic that God describes the action of consuming wine in Proverbs 23:32, "At the last it biteth like a serpent, and stingeth like an adder"? The cautionary descriptions do not work for a coral snake, the most venomous snake in the world. It has round pupils. However, if you get close enough to the coral snake to determine the pupil structure, it is too late for your safety. You are already bitten! The same goes for alcohol.

There is not one passage in the Bible in which God smiles on consuming alcoholic *yayin* or oinos. "Wait," you say! "I think I know some passages that gives God's permission to drink alcohol!" Stick with the rest of the book because we will deal with those passages in your mind and some passages that disturb my mind, those that seemingly interfere with the analysis and conclusions of this chapter. We will examine specifically where wine was used in the Old Testament sacrificial offerings, and where gladness seems to be associated with drinking alcoholic wine. Read on if you're serious about discovering the truth, but surely you have to confess at this point that wine is not always wine, as we think about it, in many places of God's word.

Chapter Two

When Noah and Lot Got Drunk

Two of the most shocking stories about alcohol consumption appear in Genesis 9 and Genesis 19. These stories are so scandalous you would think that Moses would have been embarrassed to include them in the canon of Scripture. Yet, man has no control over that. Scripture says in 2 Peter 1:21 that "holy men of God spake as they were moved by the Holy Ghost." The word "moved" in the Greek means to "be carried along." The men who wrote Scripture were simply obedient to the Holy Spirit's leading on what was to be written. This fact is important for the conclusion of this chapter and will help us understand why God would allow such stories to be given in the Holy Book from Heaven.

Noah was the ninth patriarch from Adam. His grandfather was Methuseleh, who lived to be 969 years of age, the longest lifespan recorded in scripture. It was the year that Methuseleh died that the flood came, in 1656 AM (anno mundi - meaning "the year of the world), or 2348 B.C. In Genesis 6, God describes Noah with four notable phrases: "found grace in the eyes of the Lord"; "a just man"; "perfect in his generations"; and "walked with God." In this passage God also states that all the world had become corrupt, and there was only one man in whom He could find favor and save his family from a worldwide burial in water. This flood judgment would wipe out the human race except for the eight souls in Noah's family (1 Peter 3:20).

Noah was a just man. However, this does not mean he was perfect and without sin. Oh no, every man and woman since Adam have "sinned and come short of the glory of God." Romans 5:12 plainly states, "Wherefore, as by one man sin entered into the world, and death by sin; and so death passed upon all men, for that all have sinned." Noah, however, was commended by God to be a man who with all intent lived a righteous life in his conduct and character. In comparison to the lawless, wicked, violent population that surrounded Noah, those who God describes as having "every imagination of the thoughts of their hearts were only evil continually," Noah was CONSIDERED righteous in the eyes of God. Keep that thought in mind. No man ever "earns" grace by self-righteousness. All men can "find" grace when God comes to save them because God, in the moment of salvation, looks beyond our sins to view us as righteous through the blood of Christ. How crucially important is this fact when the Bible records a terrible stain upon Noah's life after he exits the ark!

The Genesis account also says Noah was "perfect in his generations." This cannot refer to having righteous kids since we'll soon discover one child mocked Noah and took great pleasure in knowing that his father had transgressed the will of God by drinking alcohol. This description of generational perfection has much to do with the indication that there were giants in the land due to the "sons of God came in unto the daughters of men, and they bare children to them."(Genesis 6) Once again Satan is seeking to corrupt, destroy, and ruin the heredity of man, the DNA of the human race, in order to foul God's redemptive plan. Gaebelein asserted:

> The theory that 'sons of God' must mean pious people can likewise not be sustained. The term sons of God is never applied in the Old Testament to believers. ...The result of the marriage of the sons of God with the daughters of men were children, who were heroes, men of the Name. If the sons of God were simply the pious Sethites, who mixed with the Cainites, it is hard to understand why the offspring should be a special race, heroes, men of the Name. The giants were Nephilim, which means 'the fallen ones.' Sons of God is the term applied in the Old Testament to supernatural beings, both good and evil.[8]

---

[8]Arno C. Gaebelein, *Gaebelein's Concise Commentary on the Whole Bible* (Neptune: Loizeaux Brothers, 1985), 21. (See also M. R. Dehaan, *Signs of the Times*, pp. 124-132 and I. D. E, Thomas, The Omega Conspiracy, pp. 83-106.)

But there was one man, whom God would use to perpetuate the generations so that it would be possible to bring forth Jesus Christ, the Saviour of the world as the progeny of a God-fearing family.

There is great rejoicing in the divine description of Noah's life: "Noah walked with God." Noah's great grandfather Enoch did that also, and God rewarded him with a translation to heaven without death. (See Genesis 5:24) These admirable qualities of Noah's life are set as the backdrop of the flood and the ark of salvation. Using Genesis chapters 6 through 8, we learn several facts about the patriarch. Noah was on the ark for approximately 370 days. He was called by God into the ark when he was 600 years old. That would make him 601 years old when he came off the ark. He lived to be 950 years at the point of his death. So, Noah's flood experience came at the point when he had lived two-thirds of his life. In comparison to the modern day lifespan of 80 years, Noah would have been like a 53 year old person when he left the ark. We often speak of living long enough to "know better." However, Proverbs 16:31 says, "The hoary head is a crown of glory, IF IT BE FOUND IN THE WAY OF RIGHTEOUSNESS." Old age, with the accompanying grey or white hair, doesn't always guarantee "good sense," much less wisdom. Even though Job 12:12 says, "With the ancient is wisdom; and in length of days understanding," we also encounter a rebuttal in Job 32:9, "Great men are not always wise: neither do the aged understand judgment." Even the seasoned soul can fall into sin! This was the case with Noah.

The Biblical account describes Noah as becoming a farmer, literally a "ground man" when he exited the ark. Genesis 9:20 declares, "And Noah began to be an husbandman, and he planted a vineyard." However, Noah's transgression was not in growing grapes but in the use of the agricultural product. Some try to make a case that before the flood, there was a vapor canopy overhead called the "firmament" that was broken in the flood. The argument is that the vapor canopy before the flood filtered the sun's rays thereby preventing the possibility of fermented wine before the flood. Henry Morris lays that speculation to rest: "some writers have suggested that the different atmospheric conditions before the Flood somehow inhibited the decay process, but there seems to be no reasonable scientific basis for this idea."[9] Fresh grape juice does not depend solely on the radiation of the sun to make fermented wine. Noah, as described in Genesis 9:21, got drunk, got naked, and was openly exposed to anyone who walked into his tent. Drinking alcohol breaks down inhibitions so that a man will lose his decency. Adam hid because he was ashamed of his nakedness. (See Genesis 3:10) Noah, as an old man exposed himself, proving the shameful effects of drinking alcohol. But the worst was yet to come.

Noah's second son, Ham, discovered his father's shameful inebriation. Genesis 9:22 says, "And Ham, the father of Canaan, saw the nakedness of his father." The word "saw" (Hebrew *ra'ah*) means to gaze upon with enjoyment and satisfaction. Some try to make a homosexual intent out of Ham's vision of his father but it is far more likely that Ham rejoiced to see his father's sinful failure. Morris again provides a cogent explanation of what really was happening:

> "A much more probable interpretation of Ham's actions here is that they expressed a long-hidden resentment of his father's authority and moral rectitude. There was apparently a carnal and rebellious bent to Ham's nature, thus far restrained by the spiritual strength and patriarchal authority of his father. Now, however, beholding the evidence of his father's human weakness before his very eyes, he rejoiced, no doubt feeling a sense of release from all the inhibitions which had unto now suppressed his own desires and ambitions."[10]

Clear evidence of Ham's evil motivation is found in his subsequent action of running out to tell his brothers the salacious news rather than covering his father's nakedness out of respect. It delighted Ham to see his father fail and degrade himself. This disrespect for authority is the way of many a young person excusing their drinking alcohol. Their immediate claim is "but look who else is doing it," as if that makes it right in God's eyes.

---

[9]Henry M. Morris, *The Genesis Record* (Grand Rapids: Baker Book House, 1976), 234.

[10]Ibid, 235.

In contrast to Ham's shameful delight, Shem and Japheth walked backward with a blanket and covered the nakedness of their father. When Noah awoke from his drunkenness he was aware of what Ham had done and he pronounced a prophetic curse upon Ham's son, Canaan. That doesn't seem right does it? Perhaps there is a missing detail in the story. Could it be possible that Canaan was there also to poke fun at his grandfather's sin? We have no way of telling. What we know for sure is that God's way never makes the son pay for the father's sins. We read in Deuteronomy 24:16, "The fathers shall not be put to death for the children, neither shall the children be put to death for the fathers: every man shall be put to death for his own sin." Again in Ezekiel 18:20 we read, "The soul that sinneth, it shall die. The son shall not bear the iniquity of the father, neither shall the father bear the iniquity of the son: the righteousness of the righteous shall be upon him, and the wickedness of the wicked shall be upon him." So, maybe Canaan was there also to poke fun at his grandfather's sin. Furthermore, we must conclude that Noah's prophecy was directed by God because the line of Ham was already corrupted in their youth, as witnessed already in his son Canaan. Even in Noah's stupor there was vision provided by the Holy Spirit that overcame the intoxicating spirits.

Scripture validates Noah's prophecy, as revealed in the recorded history, that the Canaanites were wicked people following the fertility cults of the day and participated in everything unimaginable and perverse. They truly became the "slave of the slaves," and Noah's prophetic curse upon this side of his family was fulfilled according to Joshua 9:23, "Now therefore ye are cursed, and there shall none of you be freed from being bondmen, and hewers of wood and drawers of water for the house of my God." The descendants of Ham became menial servants to the descendants of Shem during the days of the temple worship. They were "hewers of wood and drawers of water." Man seeks to elevate himself above authority in his life and excuse moral decay in his heart. The result is that God humbles him.

The case of Lot's drunken scene is far worse than Noah's. Genesis 19 relates the story. Lot had already lost his witness because of his compromised morals. Two angels came to warn Lot to flee Sodom and Gomorrah because both these cities were scheduled for Divine demolition and destruction due to their sin of violent homosexuality. The perverts of the town had come to Lot's house, seeing the angels entering the house, and tried to break down the door to sodomize the Heavenly strangers. Lot begged them not to do such wickedness but offered them the less wicked option of taking his daughters for sex. How could a father do that? Surely these daughters heard their dad's proposal and never forgot it. In fact, the day came when these daughters would conspire to make Lot pay for his compromise against them.

After the angels thwarted off the perverts, they commanded Lot and his family to flee to the mountains. Lot left Sodom with his two daughters, lost his wife on the way, and came to the city of Zoar. Zoar lay between Admah and Zeboim to the north and Sodom and Gomorrah to the south. Everybody in that area that survived the destruction knew of the Lot's escape. Obeying the angels' original command, Lot took his daughters and lived in the mountains. These were the mountains in the area of the Dead Sea, and they had many habitable caves. The prosperity of the valley below had suddenly been buried in a grave of Divine judgment, and the passage says that Lot was fearful. His daughter's were fearful also but for a different reason than their dad. They feared never having a husband and never having children. Obviously, they felt their father was a morally compromised man for the scene in Sodom but they also knew that Lot was a God-fearing man in that he obeyed the instructions of God to save his life and his daughter's lives. They knew that what they were conspiring to do in order to become pregnant would never happen without getting their father so drunk he would not realize what he was doing.

Genesis 19:32 begins the heinous and hideous account of the incest. "Come, let us make our father drink wine, and we will lie with him, that we may preserve seed of our father. And they made their father drink wine that night: and the firstborn went in, and lay with her father; and he perceived not when she lay down, nor when she arose." The second daughter did the same thing the very next night, and both had boy children by their own father.

Notice two things about this scandalous account. First of all, in spite of the fact that nearly everything was lost in Sodom - possessions, political position, the death of Lot's wife and two sons - these girls had brought alcohol from Sodom to get their father drunk. Do you think that the girls had this planned all along, once they heard of the bad news? One thing is for sure, they could lose all, but they wouldn't give up their alcohol!

How the human race never changes. People give up their families, their possessions, their good-paying jobs, their dignity, and their freedom in order to keep their booze. It makes little sense, but that is the soul-damning, mind-numbing, senseless truth about wine and strong drink. Proverbs 20:1 says, "Wine is a mocker, strong drink is raging: and whosoever is deceived thereby is not wise." Alcohol makes a fool out of a person. The drinker will do stupid things under the influence. I have personally watched this happen regardless of whether the drinker has had a little or had too much. The quantity does not matter, only the influence. It is an evil influence. By simple availability, alcohol influenced these two daughters of Lot to violate God's law in order to get what they wanted. The result was devastating.

The offspring of this incestuous, drunken affair were Ammon and Moab. The Ammonites and the Moabites became a plague to the tribe of Israel. The Moabites did everything they could to block Israel's expansion from Canaan. The Moabite king, Balak, called upon the false prophet Balaam to curse Israel (See Numbers 22-24). The Ammonites were likewise guilty for not letting Israel pass through their land after they left Egypt (See Deuteronomy 23:4-5). You can read of numerous battles Israel had with the Ammonites and Moabites in 2 Samuel 8 and 1 Chronicles 19. These were the "cousins of Israel" through Abraham's nephew, Lot. In 1 Chronicles 19 you'll read of a shameful reaction within the camp of the Ammonites against David's army. David and king Nahash of the Ammonites were good friends and allies but Nahash had died. His son, Hanun, spread lies about David's army and the Ammonites cut off the beards of the servants of David and also cut off their britches to expose their buttocks. This angered David and soon God gave him victory in defeating the Ammonites.

Such are the Bible stories of Noah and Lot. Why are these stories in the Bible? Because God has never sought to cover up the sins of righteous men. These histories are in the Bible for the same reason we find a record of Abraham lying about his wife, a detailed account of David's adultery with Bathsheba, the account of Jonah's rebellion which allowed him to spend a few night's in the belly of a great fish, as well as countless others.

God wants us to see that there is a penalty to pay for ignoring His word. Contrary to popular opinion, the Bible does not having anything positive to say about drinking wine and strong drink. Instead the Bible demonstrates horrible outcomes from alcohol as exemplified in Bible characters. These deleterious effects will cross generational lines where children, who fail to see the evil of alcohol, reap the destruction over and over again. Yet, some in the Bible did not touch the "devil's brew" and that is the subject of our next chapter.

Chapter Three

Condemned By Example

We have already looked at the examples of Noah and Lot. Believe it or not there are other negative examples of alcohol consumption in the Bible giving further conclusive evidence that God despises it. Let us examine a few to be convinced of the truth: God hates beverage alcohol.

Probably the most famous case of a drunken party is that of Belshazzar in Daniel 5. "Belshazzar the king made a great feast to a thousand of his lords, and drank wine before the thousand." This text uses a new word for wine, *chemer*, which was defined in Chapter One as an intoxicating drink. *Chemer* is only used 7 times in the Old Testament and it is an Aramaic word. Since this word is used in Deuteronomy 32:14, expressed in the words of "pure blood of the grape," a question arises as to whether it refers to fermented wine or not. However, given that Deuteronomy 32:38 repeats some of the phrasing in verse 14 and uses the word *yayin*, intoxicating wine, they are one in the same. That conclusion is affirmed when Belshazzar's moral restraints were so loosened to bring out the sacred temple vessels, captured from Israel, and commit sacrilege by worshiping other gods while drinking alcohol from these vessels. God was so angered at the act that it cost Belshazzar his life and kingdom that very night.

Alcohol loosens a man's inhibitions. I was serving as a waiter in a steakhouse during my college days and a couple came in that were obviously drunk. When I came to their table to take their order the man began to try and expose the upper anatomy of his female companion and call my attention to it all. I walked away as she was slapping his hand. But the woman was also grinning. She, too, was drunk and loose in her morals. I simply did not stay around to find out the next thing the man or woman would do under the influence of alcohol. Their behavior in that public place incensed me.

Some might foolishly argue that Belshazzar's sin was not in drinking the intoxicating wine but in defiling the sacred vessels of Jerusalem's Temple with the wine. That is like the modern adage, "you shouldn't drink and drive," as if driving under the influence is the major problem. There would be no problem in Belshazzar's day or in our day if people didn't numb their mind with the cursed alcohol. However, the feast in Belshazzar's court reminds me of the phrase in the book of Amos where God says, "for three transgressions and for four" He will not turn back the punishment. Belshazzar had gotten to number four, but God was already angry with the first three: his pride, his arrogance, and his drinking. The fourth transgression, wine-drinking from Jehovah's vessels to worship other gods, put it over the edge. God wrote the Chaldean's death certificate that night.

Even in Bible times alcohol has been used for clandestine purposes. The most grievous story of subterfuge in all the Old Testament is found in 2 Samuel 11. David commits adultery with Bathsheba. Bathsheba sends word to the king's palace that she is pregnant. David tells his army general to send Bathsheba's husband, Uriah, home from the battle. David orders Uriah to go home for the night. Uriah, unaware of the violation the king had made to his home, sleeps outside the king's door in the servant's quarters. In the morning David finds this out, and so to cover up his sin of adultery, tries again to make Uriah go home to sleep with his wife. This time he gets Uriah drunk, but Uriah still sleeps outside the palace and doesn't go home. Then David ensures Uriah is killed on the battlefield through orders given to Joab. David knew that alcohol had the capacity to deaden Uriah's intelligence level and manipulate a cover up for sin. David paid a high price for this evil action. He lost the baby conceived in adultery. His two sons, Amnon and Absalom, became mortal enemies till Amnon was killed. Absalom died hanging in a tree by the sword of Joab. Adonijah, another son, was killed by Solomon in a political dispute. Nathan prophesied that David's wives would be humiliated before all Israel (see 2 Samuel 12:11). This found fulfillment in Absalom sleeping with many of David concubines (see 2 Samuel 16:22). Bitter fruits come with the sins of adultery and drinking alcohol.

Another example comes in the year 877 B.C. when the northern kingdom of Israel had a new king. His name was Elah, the son of Baasha. 1 Kings 16 gives the account. "In the twenty and sixth year of Asa king of Judah began Elah the son of Baasha to reign over Israel in Tirzah, two years." Normally a king ruled till he died but this would not be true for the "posterity" of Baasha. Baasha, according to 1 Kings 16:2, followed in the ways of Jeroboam, which was the idolatrous worship of Baal. Jehu, the prophet, declared that God would destroy the dynasty of Baasha. This is why Elah only ruled two years. However, prophetic judgment was not the only call of demise in Elah's kingdom. 1 Kings 16:9 indicts Elah as a drinker. "And his servant Zimri, captain of half his chariots, conspired against him, as he was in Tirzah, drinking himself drunk in the house of Arza steward of his house in Tirzah." Again we see alcohol as the catalyst for catastrophe. Elah never saw it coming. "And Zimri went in and smote him, and killed him, in the twenty and seventh year of Asa king of Judah, and reigned in his stead." Alcohol has the power to take all you have, including your life.

King Ahasuerus of Persia divorced his wife, the queen Vashti, because she refused to sully her royal respect by submitting to her husband's decree that she come into the chamber where all the king's men and the king himself was drunk. A quick read of Esther 1 shows the king's foolishness and drunken debauchery in shaming his wife rather than protecting her. Yet, God demonstrates through the account that upon man's foolishness the providential plan of God is never thwarted. Esther replaced Vashti. Be not deceived, however, into thinking an alcoholic party is a good thing. The plan of God is better to be boosted on the shoulders of righteousness than evil.

Hosea 3:1 implies that one reason Gomer was pulled into prostitution was her love of "flagons of wine." Joel 3:3 speaks of a time when God will deal with the nations who have dealt treacherously with Israel. The specific charges are they, "have given a boy for an harlot, and sold a girl for wine." Evil pleasure meant more than respectable living.

When Nahum prophesied against Ninevah, which had long since departed from the revival fires in the day of Jonah, Nahum wanted the Ninevites to know that the Lord is good, merciful, and "knows those who trust him." But Nahum 1:10 clearly pointed out that "while they are drunken as drunkards" the fire of God's judgment will burn them up like dry stubble. Thus we see three Minor Prophets, Hosea, Joel, and Nahum, forcefully warn about God's disfavor of alcohol. How can anyone presume that God has given His approval of drinking the intoxicating beverage when so much indictment for judgment appears in Scripture against it?

The fact of drunken preachers in Isaiah's day just maximizes the argument of heaven against alcohol. "His watchmen are blind: they are all ignorant, they are all dumb dogs, they cannot bark; sleeping, lying down, loving to slumber. Yea, they are greedy dogs which can never have enough, and they are shepherds that cannot understand: they all look to their own way, every one for his gain, from his quarter. Come ye, say they, I will fetch wine, and we will fill ourselves with strong drink; and to morrow shall be as this day, and much more abundant" (Isaiah 56:10-12). It is one thing for preachers themselves to fall into sin and quite another to invite others into their abominable ways. The reason these lazy, backslidden preachers were defying God is that they had no fear of God and believed that "tomorrow shall be as this day, and much more abundant." Just because sinful pursuits have not met with punitive judgment today doesn't mean it is safe to continue the sinful course tomorrow. Why? Because the fool who said the same thing in Luke 12:12 was quickly notified, "this night thy soul shall be required of thee: then whose shall those things be, which thou hast provided?" There is a night between today and tomorrow which can stop tomorrow from coming. Watch how you live before God!

What an avalanche of evidence, seen thus far, which easily buries all notions that any portion of the Word of God approves anybody, especially Christians, to drink alcohol. It just is not there. In fact, the Bible commemorates those who did not touch the "devil's brew," as we will see in the next few chapters.

Chapter Four

The Rechabites and the Nazarites

The American Temperance Movement began in the early 19th century and one of its earliest thrusts was connected with the American Revolution. People thought the political unrest and economic distress of the times were related to alcohol abuse. Farmers in Connecticut, Virginia, and New York urged the ban of whiskey distilling. Although this movement spread to eight states, the emphasis was on temperance, not abstinence. These farmers worked to ban the production and consumption of hard spirits but not wine and beer. The American Temperance Society formed in 1826 and within 12 years claimed 8,000 local groups with a membership of 1.25 million. Their emphasis began as moral reform rather than legal measures against alcohol.[11]

Temperance societies were being organized in England about the same time with religious leaders commanding the march against alcohol. Men, like John Edgar, minister of the Presbyterian Church of Ireland, poured his stock of whiskey out his window in 1829.[12] He formed the Ulster Temperance Movement with other presbyterian clergy. His fire however was also concentrated on the elimination of hard liquor with no voice against wine and beer. In essence he threw out only part of his alcohol.

It was not until the next two decades that this "temperance movement"

---

[11]Wikipedia, "Temperance Movement,"https://en.wikipedia.org/wiki/Temperance_movement.

[12]Wikipedia, "John Edgar," https://en.wikipedia.org/wiki/John_Edgar_(minister).

would take a stronger direction towards teetotalism, the advocacy of total abstinence from consuming any kind of alcohol. Teetotalism was birthed in 1833 at Preston, England. Shockingly, an Irish Catholic priest, Theobald Matthew, formed the Teetotal Abstinence Society in 1838, yet even this movement was more politically motivated than hitched to a moral objective. The hope was to convince the English Parliament that the vast working class were worthy of voting status among the elite because of their responsible call to abstinence.[13]

Moving into the Victorian period of the 1840s, a new radical action was taken on both continents to legally prohibit the production and sale of all alcohol. Minister Jabez Tunicliff formed the *Band of Hope* in 1847 for the purpose of campaigning politically against pubs and brewers. They also were socially militant in rescuing the youth from the evils of alcohol use. Their biggest drive was to get as many people possible to sign their "Pledge of Allegiance" to the abstinence society which stated, "I abstain from all liquors of an intoxicating quality whether ale, porter, wine or ardent spirits except as medicine."[14] From there the temperance/total abstinence movement exploded. Baptist missionary, Joseph Gelson Gregson, in 1862, organized the Soldier's Total Abstinence Association in British India.[15] In 1864, Methodist William Booth organized the Salvation Army with a heavy emphasis on abstinence from alcohol, plus majoring on social ministries for community support.

This history is enlightening, revealing that the call for abstinence came from Methodists, Irish Catholics, and Presbyterians alike. Their modern counterparts, for the most part, are social drinkers having no conscience to abstain. Surely, this historical portrait begs the following questions: for what and how long does it take for a person, who claims to be a Christian, to completely abandon "abstinence convictions" about alcohol? How long does it take a denomination to waffle on the truth?

---

[13] Wikipedia, "Temperance Movement."

[14] Iain Gately. *Drink: A Cultural History of Alcohol* (New York: Gotham Books, 2009) 248.

[15] Wikipedia, "Temperance Movement."

One of the "Friendly Societies" promoting abstinence organized during the Prohibition days was the "Independent Order of Rechabites" founded in 1842 stateside.[16] This order provided membership for males and females age 16-55 who would sign a pledge of teetotalism. That society still exists as a financial institution with the same name, but today it concentrates on providing ethical savings and investment products not tied to entities which promote alcohol, arms, tobacco, gambling, and pornography industries.

Where did that name "Rechabites" come from? Straight from the Bible in Jeremiah 35. Though relatively unfamiliar, it is a name worthy of any person's study. I have to confess that I had overlooked this passage and these special people until the 1970s while attending seminary. Therefore, it is not surprising that vast numbers of Christians who have been in church most of their life have never heard of the Rechabites. Let's examine the account as recorded in Jeremiah 35:1-19.

Jeremiah, the 7th century prophet to the southern kingdom of Judah, was told by God to go to the house of the Rechabites, bring them into the house of the Lord, and offer them wine to drink. The wine that Jeremiah is to offer these Rechabites in the house of the Lord, in the chamber of the descendants of Igdaliah, a very holy man of God, was real fermented, alcoholic wine. It is the Hebrew word *yayin* in that passage. Oh, now, lest the beer guzzlers and wine bibbers jump on that fact and start claiming God is in cahoots with the brewers and promoting alcohol consumption, just wait one righteous minute while we set the record straight. There was a holy reason why God gave such instruction to Jeremiah.

God Almighty knows everything. He knew exactly what the Rechabites would do when they were offered alcoholic wine. They would refuse it. This is "show and tell" time in the school of rebellious Judah. This is a live demonstration of "Righteous Living 101." Verse 5 says, "And I set before the sons of the house of the Rechabites pots full of wine, and cups, and I said unto them, Drink ye wine" What happened next? Tension must have filled the room. The Rechabites began to speak up. "But they said,

---

[16]Wikipedia. "Independent Order of Rechabites," https://en.wikipedia.org/wiki/Independent_Order_of_Rechabites.

we will drink no wine; for Jonadab the son of Rechab our father commanded us, saying, ye shall drink no wine, neither ye nor your sons for ever." The chapter concludes with God rewarding these Rechabites for obeying their ancestor's directive. In a point of comparison, however, God promises punishment for Judah for ignoring His commands. What was the reward for this special group of abstainers in Scripture? The Rechabites would have a family descendant always serving in the temple. Judah, however, would be destroyed by Babylon.

Who are these Rechabites? These special people were descendants of Rechab, a Kenite who was related to the Midianites through Moses' father-in-law Jethro (Judges 1:16). Rechab's son, Jonadab, put the strict rules in place. His people were not to drink wine. They were not to build houses but instead live in tents. They were not to sow seed nor plant a vineyard. All of this was to preserve their holy lifestyle and traditional nomadic living connected to their ancestral tradition. This tradition was bound to the holy worship of Yahweh, the God of Israel.

At some point, the Rechabites requested to join Israel so they could follow Yahweh and worship Him. Jeremiah 35 contrasts their obedience to Israel's disobedience. This is the same Jonadab who helped Jehu rid the land of Baal worship after the reign of Ahab (See 2 Kings 10:15-17). The Rechabites were towers of strength and resolve to follow the convictions of God's Word. These were holy and consecrated people. It is certainly not a reach to say we need that kind of people in this modern world as neopaganism seeks to trap us into disobedience.

How sad it is that many sons and daughters have forsaken the righteous teaching of a godly mother or dad. Their parents would turn over in their grave to see their children touch the bottle of alcohol. They were not raised that way. Such progeny have no reverence for the Bible or a Bible-believing parent. In like manner, the Bible speaks of one Rehoboam who "forsook the counsel of the old men" (2 Chronicles 10:13). The result was the dividing of his kingdom.

How true are these words from Psalm 19:21, "There are many devices in a man's heart; nevertheless the counsel of the Lord, that shall stand." For years I have been wearied in my soul hearing all the devices man has come up with to justify drinking. It is good for the stomach (but what about the liver?). It is a good medicine. As long as I'm not drunk it is all right. That's why they make a breathalyzer, my friend, because men don't know when they're drunk and will argue the matter even with authorities. As long as I have a designated driver it is all right. Is it really all right with God? On and on, rebellious hearts proceed with the devices in their hearts, but it is the counsel of the Lord that shall stand.

What is God counseling us to know from the Rechabites? First, He holds up teetotalism as the example for God's holy people. God brags on the Rechabites! Will He brag on you when you get to heaven? Are you sure you will even get into God's Holy City when you die if you don't care about being a holy person now?

Second, these Rechabites dwelt in tents instead of houses. That means they were loosely tied to the world and thereby were able to move quickly when the enemy attacked or when it came time for God to call them home to heaven. I am not advocating a pup-tent lifestyle, just a heaven-in-focus way of life. Man is not doing much to get ready for heaven if his feet and heart are carrying the lead weights of frivolity and fixation on this world.

Recall the rich man described by Jesus in Luke 12 that was prospering, building barns to store his prosperity, and saying to himself "take thine ease, eat, drink, and be merry." The word for "drink" in that passage is the same word used in Matthew 24:49 which says, "and to eat and drink with the drunken." The "certain rich man" had forgotten about the brevity of life and began to live a loose life with all his buddies who drank alcohol. Jesus said of this man, "Thou fool, this night thy soul shall be required of thee: then whose shall those things be, which thou hast provided?" The next words on Christ's lips forewarned all generations to come. "So is he that layeth up treasure for himself, and is not rich toward God" (Luke 12:20-21). If a man or woman is rich toward God they will be free from the pull of alcohol and a covetous lifestyle.

Third, the Rechabites, in their holy living, were preparing for heaven. There are no drunkards in heaven (see 1 Corinthians 6:9-10). There are no pubs, breweries, beer joints, wineries, package stores, or drinking parties in heaven because Revelation 21:27 says, "there shall in no wise enter into it any thing that defileth." Alcohol by its very nature is defiled and corrupted. The sweet has soured. The delightful has decayed. Only changed lives who have repented of such defilement will go to the Father's house. If you expect to meet the Rechabites in heaven, your belief and behavior concerning alcohol must match theirs in holiness. Obedience to God is evidence of a changed life. Let not your lips touch the stuff. Be proud to be a teetotaler.

There was a second group in the Bible that practiced teetotalism. They are called the Nazarites. The first mention of their kind is found in Numbers 6. God said to Moses, "Speak unto the children of Israel, and say unto them, When either man or woman shall separate themselves to vow a vow of a Nazarite, to separate themselves unto the LORD: He shall separate himself from wine and strong drink, and shall drink no vinegar of wine, or vinegar of strong drink, neither shall he drink any liquor of grapes, nor eat moist grapes, or dried." In addition to the prohibition on alcohol or even fresh fruit that could sour in the stomach, the Nazarite vow prohibited the cutting of the hair, and he could not defile himself by coming in contact with a dead corpse, or a grave, even if it was family members.

The Nazarite vow was practiced by either sex, since we discover that Samson's mother also vowed the vow during her pregnancy with him (See Numbers 6:2 and Judges 13:4, 14). This was a vow of separation and consecration to God as well as a separation from the world and the lifestyle of the average citizen. The obligation could be for a defined duration or for life. For the women it was a vow that could be nullified by a father or a husband. The word Nazarite could come from the Hebrew *nezer*, which means diadem, or it could come from *nazar*, which means to separate. It could be both since the hair is considered the crown (See Proverbs 16:31 and 1 Corinthians 11:15). The Nazarite would be viewed as a "crowned one," as Numbers 6:7 says, "the consecration of his God is upon his head."

The vow of the Nazarite was not a lazy vow in which a person withdrew from all duties of citizenship. On the contrary, the Nazarite continued his flow and involvement with the rest of the world. He modeled the teachings of Christ from John 17:14-16 in which Jesus challenges us to be "in the world" but not "of the world." This fact is significant for us today. While we are exposed to alcohol, we do not have to drink it.

Three important things about the Nazarite vow should be noted. Samson had a permanent vow which meant he would follow the dictates of this vow for his whole life. Yet, Samson broke the vow in all three points of the Nazarite requirement. He fooled around with Delilah till she found the secret of his God-given power. Samson said it was in his hair. The power was not in his hair, the symbol of his consecration. The power was in his sustained commitment to the vow, which he broke in the revealing of the secret to a forbidden woman in his life. Delilah was a Philistine. Samson was sent by God, the consecrated Defender and Deliverer of Israel from the Philistine yoke. He gave in to the enemy.

When you flirt with the enemy you have broken your vow to God and will suffer the consequences. Is drinking alcohol equivalent to flirting with the enemy? There is no doubt that it is because it breaks the vows of consecration in the life of a Christian that says at salvation your body becomes the property of God and the temple of the Holy Ghost (See 1 Corinthians 6:19-20). God calls His people to the highest standards of holiness, the same holiness of the Rechabites and Nazarites. The least that you can lose by drinking alcohol is the loss of your Christian witness. Do you dare to think that people who see you turn the booze bottle up to your lips will continue to think you are a holy child of God who has consecrated your life and your body to the Lord? Only a confused mind would believe that!

The second crucial point of Samson's infidelity to the Nazarite vow occurred when he came into contact with a dead body, the lion that he slew and touched it when he took honey out of the carcase. He did that out of pride to toy with the Philistines with his riddles. The Bible says that "Pride goeth before a fall" (Proverbs 16:18). It takes some measure of pride for a Christian to drink alcohol and believe that God still favors such a life.

The third violation of Samson's vow took place when he disregarded the first commitment of the Nazarite. Did Samson drink wine after he took the Nazarite vow? Judges 14:10 seems to imply that he did. "So his father went down unto the woman: and Samson made there a feast; for so used the young men to do." The Hebrew word for "feast" is *mishteh*, which literally means a drinking feast, party, banquet. It's the same kind of feast that Isaac threw for Abimelech when he flirted with the enemy and the

Philistine king's men got drunk at that feast (Genesis 26). It is the same kind of feast that Nabal threw in his house and his " heart was merry within him, for he was very drunken" (1 Samuel 25:36). It is the same kind of "feasting" that Job 1:4 says the righteous patriarch's sons and daughters were doing. They were drinking alcohol and Job sensed it. That is why he was praying for them every day because in Job's own words, "It may be that my sons have sinned, and cursed God in their hearts."

Godly, praying parents sense in their heart that the kids are turning away from God, turning to alcohol, turning to drugs, turning to a lustful, partying lifestyle. Thank God for praying parents. Thank God that in his mercy He still used Samson to destroy the Philistines even though the boy had broken with impunity the Nazarite vow. Life was shortened for this Hebrew boy named Samson because He would not stay true to God. How about your life? Are you staying true, clean and "pure, unspotted from the world" (James 1:27). If not, the Scripture says you do not have "pure religion and undefiled." Social drinker or party animal, there is no difference in the eyes of God! Clean up your vow, dear Christian, if you have broken it!

Again, why would God put these two examples of teetotalism in the Bible if He did not mean to broadcast the message, "God's best people do not touch alcohol." You cannot stay sober in mind, body and spirit if you drink the foul brew. It is meant to defile you. It is meant to ruin your testimony. It is meant to overpower your consecration to God. You don't have to be a falling down, three-sheets-to-the-wind drunkard to displease God. Just bring a beer to your table and one day He'll tell you what He thinks of it. Just stock wine in your refrigerator at home where you think you can imbibe in secret and one day He'll let you know what He thinks about it face-to-face. In the meantime why don't you consider that He's already let you know, by the Rechabites and the Nazarites, what He thinks about it! Great shame will come to you if you continue drinking and wait to find out God's view at the judgment bar when you already have that understanding from Scripture now.

Chapter Five

Solomon on Booze

Few church members are aware that the Jewish King David had nineteen sons. Anyone who is a Bible student is likely familiar with the sons Adonijah, the usurper to the throne; Amnon, who raped his half-sister Tamar; Absalom, who avenged his sister's rape by killing Amnon; and the son that Bathsheba bore to David by adultery which died. Almost all Bible students are familiar with the tenth son to David, heir to the throne of Jerusalem, king Solomon. They are also familiar with Solomon's request to God for wisdom and the quintessential display of that wisdom when he ascertained the true biological mother of a child by calling for the dismemberment of the child. All of this information is available for Bible readers in 1 Kings 3. But, if you are surprised that David had nineteen sons is it possible that you have limited knowledge on what the Bible says about drinking alcohol? Could it be that those who think the Bible supports the drinking of alcohol are simply ignorant of the Scriptures? I have maintained for many years that one of the great sins of the Church is Biblical illiteracy. A critical place in the Bible where Scripture is ignored, concerning alcohol, is the wisdom books of the Old Testament.

God considered Solomon a credible penman for sacred Scripture despite his many flaws. Commanded to never intermarry with heathen brides, this king still took 700 wives and 300 concubines (See 1 Kings 11:3). The passage indicates his wives turned away his heart from God. Anything or anyone that turns a person's heart away from God is no friend to the soul. Evil behavior is contagious but it is still evil in the eyes of God despite widespread acceptance in the culture and custom. Wine and women have ruined many lives, especially rulers. Did Solomon have anything wise to say about the dangers of drinking alcohol? Did God allow him the privilege of writing three books in the Old Testament to reveal anything about God's view on drinking alcohol? Yes! We find evidence in all three books written by Solomon.

Proverbs is the richest treasure of God's stance against alcohol consumption. Three wise discussions suffice to show without a doubt God is not permissively smiling at alcohol consumption. Proverbs 20:1 declares the stupidity of drinking alcohol. "Wine is a mocker and strong drink is raging: and whosoever is deceived thereby is not wise." Solomon says *yayin* (fermented) wine mocks the drinker. In this verse, the perpetrator is inanimate, an object, wine. It does not point the finger first at the drinker but the drink. The purpose of this wisdom is to make the human race aware of the inherent, built-in dangers of alcohol. It is not about abuse. It is about using even a small amount and the user is forewarned. Wine will mock you. Wine will hold you in derision. Wine will laugh at your foolishness in being a participant. Strong drink is the Hebrew *shekar* which Unger identifies as "an intoxicant...inebriating drink" therefore including "liquor obtained from barley."[17] The modern day equivalent to the alcoholic barley drink in Solomon's day is beer. *Shekar* is "raging." Raging referred to the growling of a bear or the snarling of a dog.

Solomon's point was to show the fearful backlash of drinking alcohol. It is a substance that will growl back at you with a great roar. Alcohol, once imbibed, will not leave you alone. It threatens you and snarls at you. That is certainly not the glamorous image the breweries publicize. But Proverbs 20:1 is God's billboard designed to prevent His creation from doing something stupid. There is a stark contrast between Proverbs 20:1 and the opponent's incessant praise for party booze. Instantly you should take away from this one simple proverb that when someone issues you the invitation to drink alcohol or provides it at a party, they are in essence saying, "Let us be idiots." Billy Sunday, the great evangelist who called people to get on the "water wagon" (trade their booze for water) said:

---

[17]Merrill F. Unger, *Unger's Bible Dictionary*(Chicago: Moody Press, 1957), 1168.

The saloon is a liar. It promises good cheer and sends sorrow. It promises health and causes disease. It promises prosperity and sends adversity. It promises happiness and sends misery. Yes, it sends the husband home with a lie on his lips to his wife; and the boy home with a lie on his lips to his mother; and it causes the employee to lie to his employer. It degrades. It is God's worst enemy and the Devil's best friend.[18]

Sunday's opinion mirrors Solomon's description of alcohol. Does that wisdom sound like God favors alcohol for a moment? The undisputed answer is no!

Proverbs 23 speaks of the sinister addiction of alcohol. Guess what Solomon said the drinker of alcohol will receive? Verse 21 says he will reap poverty. Verse 29 says he will obtain woe, sorrow, contentions, babbling, wounds without cause, and redness of eyes. Let us examine these six consequences.

All of us have woes and sorrows but who would intentionally invite such into their lives through a bottle? Contentions refers to brawling strife. Inebriated minds tend to be excessively irritable and possess a fighting spirit. Babbling accounts for the troublesome speech coming from lips bathed in alcohol which would not otherwise be spoken if the person was sober. "Wounds without cause" speaks of fights originating from alcoholic fits of rage. Redness of eyes marks the drinker who is creating a cauldron of catastrophe in their bodies by consuming alcohol.

Continuing with Solomon's wisdom, verse 31 tightens the noose around the drinker's neck. "Look not thou upon the wine when it is red, when it giveth his colour in the cup, when it moveth itself aright." When the drink is moving on its own inside the glass you are fully warned that it is a fermented drink which "bites like a serpent, and stingeth like an adder." Solomon is careful to use two different adjectives for the natural and expected operation of the snake. The first one calls attention to the hissing of the snake. The second one brings into focus the thrusting of the

---

[18]John R. Rice, *The Best of Billy Sunday*(Murfreesboro: Sword of the Lord Publishers, 1965), 76.

tongue from the poisonous viper's mouth just as it leaps to bite its victim. An argument is surely to come that "I do not go that far till it bites me." Be careful! Solomon was led of God to urge everyone not to even "look at" the wine when it is fermented, much less drink it. Now how far do you go? Do you look at wine or beer? Do you even give it a second glance as if you want it? God says don't do it!

Proverbs 31:4-5 further opens the eyes to the truth about drinking alcohol. "It is not for kings, O Lemuel, it is not for kings to drink wine; nor for princes strong drink: Lest they drink, and forget the law, and pervert the judgment of any of the afflicted." God is very clear in this text about drinking. Kings and princes, those in royal authority who daily have to make decisions concerning legal matters, must abstain from any type of alcoholic beverage. The reason is simple. Their judgment might be clouded if their brain is stupefied with alcohol and they may render the wrong judgment on the afflicted.

Solomon also included in this passage (Proverbs 31:6-7) a case of God's limited permission for alcohol. "Give strong drink unto him that is ready to perish, and wine unto those that be of heavy hearts. Let him drink, and forget his poverty, and remember his misery no more." A person who is "ready to perish" may refer either to a criminal who had been adjudicated the death penalty or a person who is in the throes of terminal illness. Even in our times, prison officials give an hallucinogen as the first injection of three in enforcing the death penalty. Hospice, hospitals, or even family are often instructed to offer wine, morphine, or some similar drug to take the harshness off the final moment of death.

The person who is of "heavy heart," taken from the Hebrew word *mar*, has a root meaning of bitterness. It is entirely proper to interpret Solomon's instruction here to be one case, not two (Verse 4 and 5 are connected to verses 6-7). The heavy heart, the bitter heart, the heart in misery, is the person who has received the death penalty or terminally ill. Yet, another sense is possible. The Hebrew *mar* indicates a bitterness that has become destructive. This understanding in no way opens the door to alcohol as medicine in every case of depression. Alcohol is a depressant. Physicians do not give depressants, but antidepressants, for depression. Modern medical advice warns of mixing depressants with alcohol because it is dangerous. Initial stages of alcohol consumption may increase dopamine levels, the body's "feel good" chemical, but continued usage can become life threatening to the central nervous system. These facts preclude Proverbs 31:6-7 from advice to take alcohol as a cure for depression. Perhaps Solomon's wisdom for the heavy hearted permitted occasional use of wine, even diluted wine, for temporary relief of psychological trauma. However, there is no permission in this passage to use alcohol indiscriminately for a psychological fix, much less a recreational drug.

There is only one other permission in the whole Bible that God gives for the use of alcohol, that given to Timothy (1 Timothy 5:23) for treating his "often infirmities." "Often infirmities" does not include daily cough syrup for someone who has developed a taste for the home brew, nor party alcohol, nor communion wine, nor after work beer, or any such. No person reading this book can rightfully twist God's Word to support the use of alcohol except for these three restricted causes: impending death, psychological trauma, and stomach infirmities.

In Ecclesiastes 2:2-3, King Solomon confesses that he traversed the party circuit, ran from entertainment to entertainment, and sought to gratify his flesh with wine in order to assess life's purpose in laughter and pleasure. His conclusion was that it was all "madness of spirit" with no accomplishment (verse 11).

Of the six times wine is mentioned in the Song of Solomon, notable are the wise king's comments that "love is better than wine," and 7:9 praised the best wine as that which "goeth down sweetly, causing the lips of those that are asleep to speak." In the first, love is for sure better than drunkenness. In the second, Solomon is referring to mixed wine (See Song of Solomon 8:3 and Isaiah 1:22). Mixed wine is the fermenting grape juice or some other fruit juice that is in the beginning stages of fermentation and the user started diluting it with water and mixing it with spices to add flavor. The difference in this *yayin* is the residual sweetness maintained by early dilution and the addition of spices. However, this in no way gives Divine endorsement of imbibing fermented wine. Solomon did a lot of things that did not garner God's favor. It simply points to the reality of alcohol's effects and the desire of the Jewish culture to dilute the fermentation with water to avoid drunkenness.

Now, there you have it. The wisest king in the Old Testament gives ample warning and specific prohibition against alcohol usage in all three books that he authored, a fact that many ignore to their detriment. It is no accident that God led Solomon to recount some of his own experiences, his own wise observations of the peril of alcohol.

The following is a true story about a member of a Church of Christ in the Nashville, Tennessee working as a patrol officer when this incident happened. It was the middle of August, a hot and muggy time around midnight, and David, the patrol officer, had been dispatched to check on a single-car accident near the Brentwood area of South Nashville. A woman passerby had seen an overturned black Jeep Wrangler, about 150 feet off the road near a sharp curve. As David came to the scene, it appeared as though the driver had taken the curve at a high rate of speed, skidded off the roadway and flipped several times. As he walked up to the Jeep, officer David felt nervous, and noted his feelings while relating the story.

"To me, vehicles look so much larger when they are upside down. There is something haunting about peering in the darkness into an overturned vehicle, looking for badly injured or deceased occupants. As I walked up to the Jeep, I noticed a lot of empty Budweiser beer cans, scattered all around. Kneeling down with my flashlight, to look under the Jeep, I didn't see anybody at first glance. Then the beam of my flashlight passed across a pair of shoeless feet. I called for a wrecker since he was pinned underneath. I gave them a Signal 10 which meant to rush it up. I pointed my beam of light directly into the young man's face. His expression appeared to be one of shock and fear. With glazed-over eyes and fixed pupils, he stared at me. But his stare had that vacant look of death. His body was there but his soul was gone."

David noticed the young man's billfold lying on the ground. We will call the young boy Zach. David learned that Zach lived less than two miles from the accident. The boy's blue jeans were wet from spilled beer. The smell was obvious. The large number of scattered cans indicated excessive consumption of alcohol.

David pulled Zach's black t-shirt down so it would cover his stomach. He couldn't believe his eyes. In big bold letters were the words "BEST

YEAR EVER!" A cold chill ran down David's spine! Then another chill ran all over his body as the medical examiner came, rolled Zach's body over, and revealed on the back of the t-shirt, also in big bold letters, one word, "BUDWEISER!" Of all the shirts Zach could have chosen to wear on his last day on earth, why did it have to be that one? His last purchase – Budweiser! His last drink – Budweiser! His last passenger with him – Budweiser! And yet in a mocking way, the words on the front of his shirt said, "BEST YEAR EVER!" Solomon was right. Booze is a mocker and a deceiver. You would be foolish to have anything to do with it.

I answered the phone one day in the study of a Kentucky pastorate. A member of the church was on the line, a distraught lady who was dear to my heart. She asked me a question that to this day has haunted me because I wondered if I gave her correct counsel. She said her husband was down sick with the flu and told her that if she didn't go out and buy his liquor he was going to get the shotgun out of the closet and kill himself. She said, "Pastor, what do I do?" No wife on planet earth should ever be faced with that kind of demand from her mate. No pastor should ever have to answer such a question.

I was sorely tempted to tell the dear Christian lady, "Tell him to shoot himself; that you're not going to buy his liquor, you ol' sot." Well, discretion held me back and I asked her another question. I called her by name and said, "Do you want to go buy his liquor?" She assured me she did not want to go to the liquor store because it would be embarrassing for her as a Christian. She told me she had never drunk alcohol, and she had never bought his alcohol. I told her that God saw her heart and very well knew that in her heart she did not want to have anything to do with her husband's sin, but if she felt she needed to be a submissive wife and regretfully go get the liquor to keep him from killing himself, I was sure that God understood her dilemma and would not hold it against her.

Did I give the right answer? I have a tendency to believe I didn't because of Habakkuk 2:15. But I determined that I would rather live with the regret of my advice than ask this lady to live with regret if her husband was hell-bent on shooting himself should she refuse to get his alcohol. Neither I nor her could have lived with that reality of him committing suicide.

This enforces King Solomon's threefold warning in Proverbs 20, 23, and 31. Proverbs 20 says alcohol will make a fool out of you. Can you think of a more glaring example of a fool than the man who threatens to shoot himself if he doesn't get his booze? Either way he is destroying himself. Proverbs 23 spotlights the sinister danger of alcohol. By the time you realize its addictive qualities it is too late to avoid the damage. Proverbs 31 highlights the great responsibility to avoid alcohol. It is not for kings. It is not for those who will maintain sensible authority in life. It matters not the quantity of alcohol drunk but moreso the hidden qualities of the drink. In the first swallow it has the capacity to plunge whole families into a living nightmare of consequences here on earth, not to even mention the judgment to come for such behavior. Have mercy, O God, and help us all to pay attention to the warnings from Solomon.

Chapter Six

Nothing Hidden, Nothing Excused

Having pastored 7 churches in 37 years, I have witnessed Biblical ignorance and illiteracy in epidemic proportions. It is inexcusable when you consider the facts. The Bible is still the number one best selling book in America for over three hundred years. Nearly every home in America has one or more copies of the Bible. Yet, people continue to show their ignorance when they stake their sole claim to drinking alcohol on this argument: "Well, Jesus made wine at the wedding, so it must be alright." They simply are oblivious to countless other passages of Scripture in God's Word that speaks to the consumption of alcoholic beverages with Divine disapproval Biblical illiteracy shouldn't be paraded. It should be corrected.

Surely and sadly the drinkers will be shocked when one day they stand before the same Jesus, whom they think contributed to the party scene by making 12 percent, intoxicating, red bubbly for the Cana wedding, who will then say to them, "Depart from me ye workers of iniquity, for I never knew you." In Chapter Eight we will prove that the Cana wine was miraculously turned from water and had no alcoholic content. Such thinking, that Jesus made alcohol, is absurd and Biblically false.

Are there any other warnings from God about drinking wine, *yayin*, or strong drink, *shekar*, by other Biblical writers? Yes! There are plentiful warnings. Let us begin with Isaiah 5:11 which says, "Woe unto them that rise up early in the morning, that they may follow strong drink; that continue until night, till wine inflame them!" Of course this is speaking of the addicted person. He rises in the morning thinking about drinking. That is addiction. He continues in the night till he is inflamed with wine.

That is addiction. We all agree that addiction is bad. But who will argue with the fact that addiction begins with participation? Many will but not me. If a man never takes a drop of wine, beer or liquor into his mouth, can he ever get addicted to alcohol? Of course not!

Isaiah 5:22 says, "Woe unto them that are mighty to drink wine, and men of strength to mingle strong drink." The word "woe" means a curse. These are the first two of four curses on drinking alcohol we will discover. The other curses, found in Proverbs 23:29 and Habakkuk 2:15, will be discussed in Chapter Eight. How many times will God have to say that alcohol has a curse with it till the drinker believes it?

Isaiah says there is a curse upon those that are "mighty to drink wine." The word "mighty" is a Hebrew word that refers to a "proud tyrant." People who drink have been known to fight by word and by fist over their drinks and their right to drink. Christians who drink beverage alcohol get angry when you try to tell them they're sinning by drinking alcohol. They spout some verse that they think will chase the teetotaler off from sounding the warning. What will they do when they stand before God whose word about the matter will be the final word? Will the "Christian drinker" argue with God then for their right to drink? Will you say to God, "But Jesus made wine"? No, the lips that imbibed the crimson curse into their body will then be silent and ashamed when they face His judgment. I believe three of those words from the Judge will be "I told you."

Isaiah 28:7 says, "But they also have erred through wine, and through strong drink are out of the way; the priest and the prophet have erred through strong drink, they are swallowed up of wine, they are out of the way through strong drink; they err in vision, they stumble in judgment." Isaiah didn't mince words. He had nothing good to say about drinking alcohol.

Daniel 1:8 is a pretty eye-opening Scripture. "But Daniel purposed in his heart that he would not defile himself with the portion of the king's meat, nor with the wine which he drank: therefore he requested of the prince of the eunuchs that he might not defile himself." The commentaries carefully reveal that Daniel's refusal to eat the king's meat and drink the king's *yayin* was because both had been offered to the idols of Babylon in worship to false gods. Daniel wanted no part of that. However, who is to say this was the only reason why Daniel refused to drink wine? Is anyone willing to take the risk of being a drinker on the basis that we do not have the same pagan rituals as Babylon? When they sell the boozin' believer a bottle of the devil's brew in the package store they do not take it in the back room and bow to ask a statue to bless it. Does that free up the backslidden hypocrite, who attends church on Sunday but passes out the liquor at his party on Monday, to drink to his heart's desire? The verse plainly says Daniel did not want to "defile" himself.

There were false gods in Daniel's day believed to be the patron gods of alcohol. One need only do a Google search to find there are over 40 liquor deities in history around the globe. Some are still worshiped today. The two main deities behind wine in Bible days were Dionysius and Bacchus. Dionysius was the Greek name, and Bacchus was the Roman name. MacArthur shed light on this cult:

> Dionysius then, according to Greek mythology, spawned a religion, a religion of ecstasy, and emotionalism. And the Dionysian cult, this religion of ecstasy and emotionalism, this frenzied kind of religion, saturated the Greek and Roman world. The Dionysian cult was a debauched form of worship. They engaged in orgies of sexual perversion, along with music and dancing and feasting. But there was one common element to all of the Dionysian debacle and that was drunkenness. In fact, if you ever circulate in the Middle East or in the ancient Roman world, you will see Dionysius associated with grapes. When there is a statue or a tribute to Dionysius, some monument to Dionysius, it is always marked out by clusters of grapes because he became known as the god of wine. The Greek name of Dionysius became in the Roman language, Latin, Bacchus. And Bacchus is the Roman god of wine. When people engaged in these unbelievable drunken brawls, they were called Bacchanalian feasts.[19]

---

[19]John MacArthur, "The Divine Pattern for Relationships," https://www.gty.org/library/sermons-library/90-97/the-divine-pattern-for-relationships.

It is clear that Daniel wanted to distance himself from anything that had to do with worship of a false god. Wine was the connector, both in Daniel's day and the present world. It connects the heart with the defilement Daniel sought to avoid. Christians should learn from Daniel's example.

Hosea 4:11 joins the parade of Scriptures that condemns the use of alcoholic wine. "Whoredom and wine and new wine take away the heart." Both primary words from the Hebrew are used in this verse, *yayin* and *tiyrowsh*. In Chapter One of this book, it was established that the terms identified an alcoholic and non-alcoholic drink respectively. So, how is it that *tiyrowsh*, according to Hosea, would presumably take away the heart from God since Hosea subsequently says Israel is a backsliding heifer? Nowhere is it denied that *tiyrowsh* cannot turn alcoholic. At first, it is simply the sweet juice of the grape. But, there is a fitting image here in Hosea. What is sweet can turn away from its original condition. It can turn sour. That is just the statement that Hosea makes in verse 18 of the same chapter. He said to Israel, "Ephraim is joined to idols: let him alone. Their drink is sour." It is a word against man's evil intent with grapes.

Isaiah 28:1 confirms Ephraim's sin: "Woe to the crown of pride, to the drunkards of Ephraim, whose glorious beauty is a fading flower, which are on the head of the fat valleys of them that are overcome with wine!" There is absolutely no reason to take this metaphorically rather than literally. The great prophet is calling attention to the fact that Ephraim's literal intoxication has moved them into literal, spiritual whoredom by offering human sacrifice to the false gods of that day. Their love of alcohol wilted them like the fading petals of a beautiful flower. It truly was a shameful departure from Almighty God resulting in the plague of drunken, orgiastic, frenzied worship of the gods of Baal. Even the leaders were infected by this wickedness. Is that not a portrait of our own country today - congressmen and leaders in high places sitting around the table with their cocktails? Why would a Christian have anything to do with a substance that is associated with such evil? Alcohol fans the flames of idolatry. Americans worship the frenzied, free lifestyle of self-indulgence. Alcohol is the vehicle that will carry this nation away from God.

Joel 1:5 takes the abstinence baton a little further down the path of righteousness. "Awake, ye drunkards, and weep; and howl, all ye drinkers of wine, because of the new wine; for it is cut off from your mouth." Drunkenness was a great problem in Israel at the time Joel wrote. Like today, people ignored many warnings from the prophets concerning drinking alcohol. In response to their drunkenness, God sent a plague of locusts to judge the people for their wicked lifestyle. Those locusts would cut a field down to nothing in a matter of minutes. The last harvest of the season was the grape harvest. Therefore, Joel was telling the people that because of their rebellion in drinking alcohol the Lord was going to cut it off at the source, the vineyard of grapes. That is why the prophet uses the phrase "new wine," which is a reference to the juice in the grape. The people of Israel would have nothing to drink from the vineyard if they were going to defile the harvest by making it alcoholic. Would to God that a plague of locusts would come today also and strip the vine of our precious grapes if we're going to continue in our rebellion with alcohol consumption!

Many have died because alcohol deadened their awareness of an approaching enemy. Amnon was easy prey for an angered half-brother Absalom bent on avenging his sister's rape. When Amnon's heart was "merry with wine" Absalom gave the order to strike him dead (see 2 Samuel 13:28-29). Asa, king of Judah, had a servant that conspired against him. That servant's name was Zimri. Asa was at Tirzah "drinking himself drunk" when Zimri, personal servant and chariot master to the king, struck him dead and took over his throne (see 1 Kings 16:8-10). When Benhadad, king of Syria, laid siege against the northern kingdom of Israel, he made a decision that weakened his position against Ahab, king of Israel. He bragged to Ahab that he was going to take all his silver, all his gold, and all his wives and children. But when you are a warrior king, there is something that will take you down faster than this act of pride. It is alcohol. In 1 Kings 20 we discover that Benhadad thought he had outnumbered Ahab's army. Boasting himself of being the victor before the battle started Scripture reveals the source of his impending defeat. It says he was "drinking himself drunk" at the noon hour with his cohorts. The battle looked impossible for Ahab to win since he only had 7,232 against Benhadad's army of over a 100,000. The outcome was that God so destroyed the armies of Benhadad that the survivors ran off from the battlefield as cowards. Benhadad barely escaped with his own life. God has given us three clear stories with a consistent message: Man is a loser when he drinks alcohol.

Deuteronomy 32:32-33 addresses rebellious Israel who were ungrateful to God for protection, provision, and guidance in the Sinai desert. Moses writes for God, "For their vine is of the vine of Sodom, and of the fields of Gomorrah: their grapes are grapes of gall, their clusters are bitter: Their wine is the poison of dragons, and the cruel venom of asps." When did Israel upset God with their ingratitude? Many times, but this incidence centers around the words in verse 17 of that passage. "They sacrificed unto devils, not to God; to gods whom they knew not, to new gods that came newly up, whom your fathers feared not." Obviously they had become involved with the Baal cult which blasphemously called for drunkenness and orgiastic frenzy to appeal to these gods.

We all know of the golden calf they made at the base of Sinai. Aaron had violated his charge given to him by his brother Moses. When the leader of Israel delayed to come down from the mountain in Sinai, the people compelled Aaron to make a golden calf modeled after the bull god Apis in Egypt. They began to say to each other, "These be thy gods, O Israel, which brought thee up out of the land of Egypt" (Deuteronomy 32:4). Gasp! Moses had praised Israel when they abstained from alcohol because such sobriety allowed greater knowledge of Jehovah. Deuteronomy 29:6 says, "Ye have not eaten bread, neither have ye drunk wine or strong drink: that ye might know that I am the LORD your God." Yet, within a short time Israel had forgotten the real God who had delivered them from their bondage in Egypt. They fell into grievous idolatry. How grievous was it? The Hebrew *shathah* (drink) in verse 6 pinpoints drinking to get drunk. Abstinence from wine increases the knowledge of the Lord, intimacy with the Creator. The opposite places a man's mind in carnal separation from the one true God. In ancient Egypt, the birth of an Apis bull resulted in a transport to the city of Memphis where for 40 days the only persons allowed to see the bull were women who exposed themselves to their new god.[20] This was the kind of worship that transpired at the base of Sinai.

There are people today who go to church but they have adopted a morality not unlike the cult of Apis the bull. They think there is abolutely

---

[20]See https://www.bible-history.com/archaeology/egypt/apis-the-bull-god.html

nothing wrong with drinking or getting drunk periodically. I pastored a church once where the city was dry but the county was wet. All 21 permits for the sale of packaged liquor were in the county seat town, just 20 miles away. When the referendum came up to provide licenses to any restaurant or other establishment intending to sell, "liquor by the drink," the local ministerial alliance met to discuss defeating the bill. How interesting that the president of the ministerial alliance, who happened to be Methodist, when nominated to be the spokesman at the city council meeting on the subject, began to resist the responsibility. The Catholic priest of our town excused himself from the discussion saying, "I have to withdraw any resistance to this measure, because as you well know drinking alcoholic beverages in the Catholic tradition is a part of our celebration." I commended him later that week for being honest but I asked the question, "Padre, what part of killing brain cells would you call a celebration?" He told me I had a very good point.

Another Methodist minister, after four hours of debate, got up and said, "Fellows, I'm a diabetic; I've got to leave and take my medicine; the way I see it - you are either for it or against it." He recognized the waffling of the parsons at the table who were more concerned with keeping their jobs than standing for righteousness. Yours truly watched the cowardly compromise in the alliance president as he addressed the council meeting, until I couldn't stand it anymore. I stood up and gave an impassioned speech of how liquor by the drink would cost them more in revenue than gain because they would be continually sweeping up the mess in more hospital staff, more ambulance staff, and more law enforcement. Later that week, I got a newspaper clipping in the mail of the reported meeting on which somebody anonymously scribbled in large red ink, "Why don't you mind your own business?" I actually thought that was exactly what I was doing, minding the business God had given me, sharing God's truth about alcohol. Isaiah 58:1 says, "Cry aloud, spare not, lift up thy voice like a trumpet, and shew my people their transgression, and the house of Jacob their sins." The minister's job is to publicly preach against sin without apology. Romans 12:9 says, "Abhor that which is evil, and cleave to that which is good."

A prominent, power-controlling deacon in the church where I pastored came to me that week and said, "Ah preacher, you just have to coexist with the liquor stores." That man is dead now, suspicioned to be in hell because of his double life. On the one hand he taught Sunday School and even preached in several churches including his own, yet he propositioned women in town hoping to get sexual favors and told dirty jokes with a gleeful look. Some people think the good they do for God will cancel out their habitual wickedness when they stand before God. This man was convinced he could live any way he desired since eternal security kept him safe. There is no eternal security like that (See Romans 6:1-2 and Matthew 7:22-23).

The deacon defended his own son who was a drunkard. He became angry when I preached on alcohol. This man, who claimed we have to coexist with the booze stores, received word one evening that his 18 year old grandson was killed by a drunk driver just months after the "liquor by the drink" passed on the ballot. I couldn't help but think about his advice to me to just let the liquor crowd do their thing while Christians coexist with the evil. He lost a grandson on the peril of that advice. How do you coexist with a killer in your town called Mr. Alcohol?

Chapter Seven

Kings and Priests

In the previous chapters, we have seen the overwhelming evidence that God does not support the consumption of alcohol. We have seen the call to abstinence through the examples of the Nazarites and the Rechabites as well as Moses' lesson that abstinence increases our knowledge of God. Yet there are more teetotalers in the Bible. Listen closely and give heartfelt attention to Leviticus 10:9-10: "Do not drink wine nor strong drink, thou, nor thy sons with thee, when ye go into the tabernacle of the congregation, lest ye die: it shall be a statute for ever throughout your generations: And that ye may put difference between holy and unholy, and between unclean and clean." This commandment was given to Aaron, brother to Moses and leader of the Tabernacle priesthood, to teach to all his generations.

To understand the background, the tribe of the Levites, of which Aaron descended through Kohath and Amram and Jochebed, were to be subordinate to the Aaronic priesthood for the menial tasks of the Temple ceremonies. Aaron was the high priest who alone had privilege to enter into the Holy of Holies on the Day of Atonement to make annual sacrifice for the sins of the nation.

Leviticus 10 records Aaron's oldest sons, Nadab and Abihu, entering into the Tabernacle's Holy Place unlawfully and offering strange fire on the Altar of Incense. Leviticus 10:2 relates the shocking response from God. "And there went out fire from the LORD, and devoured them, and they died before the LORD." It reminds me of a cereal that was popular in the 1980s - Crispy Critters. Lest you think this remark is insensitive remember this was a grievous violation against God's holiness.

Immediately on the heels of this incident Aaron was called to instruct all his priests to avoid alcohol when serving in the Temple. There is every reason to believe that Aaron and Nadab's sin is tied to alcohol consumption while serving in the Temple. Would there be any need of the instruction after the tragic event if Nadab and Abihu were sober? Gaebelein noted:

> What indeed induced them to act in this way so that the judgment of God fell upon them? The warning which follows this incident gives a strong hint on the possible cause of their presumptuous deed. Read verses 8 and 9. The warning against strong drink hints, no doubt, that they had been under the influence of strong drink. It must have been intoxication. May we remember that there is also another intoxication, which is a strange fire and which God hates.[21]

Nadab and Abihu's sin was not in violating privileges to enter the Holy Place because that was their God-given right as priests in Aaron's family. Their sin was twofold. They brought "strange fire," which meant the source of the fire was acquired somewhere other than the place God first kindled, the Brazen Altar (See Leviticus 6:13 and Leviticus 9:24). Moreover, their appalling lack of respect for God's holiness was demonstrated by their drunken state.

This conclusion is strongly supported in the prescription for service to Jehovah God, "that ye may put difference between holy and unholy, and between unclean and clean." God had already instructed, "And let the priests also, which come near to the LORD, sanctify themselves, lest the LORD break forth upon them" (See Exodus 19:22). God did break forth upon these sons of Aaron when their actions failed to set themselves apart as holy, clean, and evident men of God.

That is to be the characteristic of anyone who claims God, who professes faith in Christ, who obviously is called to be a disciple and serve the Almighty's purposes in their life. Anything less deserves the fate of Nadab and Abihu. God is holy and will not accept anything

---

[21]Gaebelein, 103.

defiled in His presence. Many Christians today violate this principle without any regard for what God says, and it surely must be the longsuffering of God waiting for their repentance that more funerals are not forthcoming.

In the Bible priests had two responsibilities. They represented God to man and interceded for man to God. First, we see Aaron was the spokesman for Moses who claimed he was "slow of tongue." When Moses received a word from God he commissioned Aaron the priest to speak it to the people. Second, Jesus Christ is our Great High Priest, who according to Paul has ascended to the right hand of God where He "maketh intercession for us" (Romans 8:34). Can you imagine a drunk Jesus praying to God for us? Can you imagine a preacher who moderately drinks, socially drinks, casually drinks alcohol claiming to be our prayer warrior? Could anyone like that have power with God? Not on your life - really! Nadab and Abihu proved that.

It is important to note that there is no double standard for preachers and the laity. All are priests unto God if they are saved. The saved life is willing to "count all things but loss for the excellency of the knowledge of Christ Jesus" and "suffer the loss of all things, and count them but dung" to "win Christ" (Philippians 3:8). Some "professed" Christians just can't give up their wine at their weddings, their beer at the ball games, and their liquor in the bedroom to win Christ. They will most certainly be denied by Christ when they need His approval the most, at the time of their death hoping to go to Heaven. They also should listen to Aaron's counsel, "that ye may put difference between holy and unholy, and between unclean and clean." How can we ever convince a lost and gainsaying world that Jesus, Heaven, and salvation is real if Christians are no different from the population of hell-bound sinners?

In addition to priests, kings are forbidden to drink alcohol. Proverbs 31:4-6 states, "It is not for kings, O Lemuel, it is not for kings to drink wine; nor for princes strong drink: Lest they drink, and forget the law, and pervert the judgment of any of the afflicted." An actual king wrote this. Some Bible scholars believe that Lemuel was a nickname given to Solomon, and this passage is a dictation of Solomon's mother to whomever Lemuel may be. God must have led the king's mother to address her son. The name Lemuel means "devoted to God" and parallels the name Solomon which means "beloved of the Lord." A man in authority over others has a sobering responsibility to render righteous judgment over those he rules. Alcohol diminishes response time and blunts the powers of reasoning. Arrests for DUIs are warranted due to the dangers of driving while intoxicated. Kings are driving a nation for the purpose of prosperity and not peril. Intoxicated kings can do great harm to others by foolish judgments. Wise kings do well to listen to godly mothers who speak for God and tell their sons to stay away from alcohol.

Does this word to kings and priests have a present parallel for Christians today? Most certainly! Revelation 1:6 says that Jesus hath made His children to be "kings and priests unto God and his Father; to him be glory and dominion for ever and ever. Amen." Revelation 5:10 repeats the heavenly identity. "And hast made us unto our God kings and priests: and we shall reign on the earth." Christians today, more than ever, are having an identity crisis. They either do not know who they are or they refuse to accept God's identification. 1 Peter 2:5,9 gives the same call: "Ye also, as lively stones, are built up a spiritual house, an holy priesthood, to offer up spiritual sacrifices, acceptable to God by Jesus Christ. But ye are a chosen generation, a royal priesthood, an holy nation, a peculiar people; that ye should shew forth the praises of him who hath called you out of darkness into his marvelous light:" Have you come out of darkness into the light? Act like it! Have you accepted the God-given role to be "kings and priests?" Live like it!

The king possessed authority. It would be a ridiculous mockery to let some substance control and govern him. Paul said in Romans 6:16, "Know ye not, that to whom ye yield yourselves servants to obey, his servants ye are to whom ye obey; whether of sin unto death, or of obedience unto righteousness?" For a Christian to drink alcohol is to declare the wrong master and the drinker becomes the foolish slave to the bottle or the goblet. Peter also wrote, "for of whom a man is overcome, of the same is he brought in bondage" (2 Peter 2:19). The principle of Christ is that "if we suffer, we shall also reign with him: if we deny him, he also will deny us" (2 Timothy 2:12). Christ even refused a necessity of life, bread, to stay true to God and His mission. Alcohol is no necessity. Alcohol is an ungodly thirst, a raging temptation, a denial of Christ, and a testimony-killing liquid. Refuse it.

We should never give up hope that Christ will change the most incorrigible drunkard. One Wednesday night, in a particular church I pastored, a deacon brought in a young man in his thirties who was quite inebriated. After the service the deacon asked me to talk to the young man. I have never refused to talk to a drunkard because my Jesus was a friend of publicans and sinners. Jesus was accused of being a winebibber and a glutton (Luke 7:34). Of course this was not true of Christ, but the criticism obviously issued out of His great kindness to sinners. Christ spent time with sinners. He did not participate in their sin. The deacon, myself and the young drinker we will call Steve went into a side room and I began to enquire of the situation. It was obvious that the young man had an alcohol problem. I soon found out that his mother, a psychologist, and his father, a very rich man had given up on their son because he was an embarrassment to them. I found out that Steve had one handsome son and another baby on the way. Steve was throwing his life away for the bottle.

I prayed in my spirit and asked God to sober Steve up enough to hear and understand the Gospel. God answered that prayer and after I thoroughly explained the Gospel of Christ and repentance Steve sincerely wanted to ask Jesus into his life. I left it up to the Lord to seal the conversion experience.

Characteristically Steve came to church for several weeks - sober and smiling. He even gave his testimony of salvation. I baptized him. Then he went missing in action for three weeks. I looked for him. His parents didn't know where he was. His wife didn't know where he was. I asked his parents, "If you had to guess where he is what would you say?" They said he probably was down at the Rusty Nail Saloon. Mind you, this preacher had never been in a saloon in his life. But I heard God say to me, as I was driving down the street where this saloon was supposed to be, "You don't need his parents' permission to go do what I need you to do."

So, I turned up a one-way street and pulled up illegally on a sidewalk because there were no parking places there. I went inside that saloon with a pace that forbade me from backing out of the God-called task. Steve was there and the bartender was sitting beside him. Both were drinking beer. Both were "lit" as they say in those circles. Steve was wide-eyed and shocked as he said, "Preacher, what are you doing here?" I replied, "Oh, no, the better question Steve is what are you doing here?" Several weeks ago you gave your life to Christ and God changed you. Now throw that beer in the trash and get up out of that chair and get out of here!" He queried, "Now?" I said, "Now. Get up and let's go. Throw that beer away."

Steve got up and we went out on the sidewalk. He was leaning on my shoulder breathing his ol' sorry booze breath in my face and said to me, "Pastor, I just don't feel worthy." I said to him, "Steve, nobody is worthy of the life-changing grace and mercy of God. But listen to this. I have three children and you have one precious blonde haired boy with another baby on the way. I don't know about you but I would not want to give up any one of my children to save the life of another. Steve, God gave His only Begotten Son, the only one He had to save you and me. That means you are worth a lot to Him, don't you think?" He replied, "I have never thought of it that way."

I took him to a detox unit and he was back in church the very next Sunday flying straight as an arrow. His mother and father were so impressed with his turn around that they started coming to church. Steve had never been sober for more than six months at a time in his life since he started drinking in his teens. When I left that pastorate he had been free from alcohol for four years. His last words to me on the subject were, "Brother Tim, God completely took the taste away from me. I don't have any desire to drink anymore."

I can only praise God for this man's deliverance. I surely hope to see him in Heaven one day. Jesus can lead anyone to be a Rechabite or a Nazarite, vowing to never drink wine or strong drink. It's a good life to live like a king and a priest unto God.

Chapter Eight

Did Jesus Really Serve Alcohol?

Jesus, His mother Mary, and Jesus' disciples attended a marriage feast in Cana of Galilee. During the feast, Jesus turned water into wine. We read of this in John 2:1-10. At the feast, the wine ran out and Mary tells Him about the problem. This furnished an opportunity for Jesus to perform His first miracle. Jesus instructed the servants to fill six water pots containing two or three firkins apiece with water . A firkin was about 9 gallons and so the combined amount of water in the pots was approximately 164-180 gallons. Now, 180 gallons of wine, the right kind of wine, would go a long way to supply plenty of refreshment to the wedding attendees. We can assume that there was a large crowd, and we can also assume that Jesus made enough wine to supply the remaining days of the feast. (The wedding feast lasted seven days while the couple were on their honeymoon.) It is entirely in the character of Christ to provide abundantly, as demonstrated in this miracle and later in the feeding of the 5000.

The one thing to note in this miracle is that the governor of the feast made a declaration about the wine. Verse 9 and 10 say, "When the ruler of the feast had tasted the water that was made wine, and knew not whence it was: (but the servants which drew the water knew;) the governor of the feast called the bridegroom, And saith unto him, Every man at the beginning doth set forth good wine; and when men have well drunk, then that which is worse: but thou hast kept the good wine until now." So, whatever kind of wine Jesus made it was deemed to be "good wine" by the governor of the feast who because of his duty would well know the quality of the product.

This miracle has been the most prominent text for those who seek to justify social drinking of alcohol. It is argued that if Jesus made wine at a wedding feast He attended, then surely He does not object to Christians drinking wine today. I will most certainly concede that if Jesus really did make alcoholic wine then no one could say that Jesus, nor His disciples, nor His mother would condemn the drinking of alcohol, but rather approve it. Therefore it is incumbent upon me, if I desire to defend the stance against drinking alcohol, to disprove any notion, no matter how loud the social drinker's voices become, to the claim that Jesus is the forerunner of the alcoholic wine industry. I must give ample proof that Jesus did not put His approval on drinking alcoholic beverages by making intoxicating wine. This is not in the least a challenging task as I relate to you the following Biblical facts.

Fact #1: If the wine at the Cana wedding previously served before Christ's miracle was alcoholic and the wine that Jesus made was alcoholic then Jesus Christ would have been supporting drunkenness.

How could that be when Ephesians 5:18 says, "And be not drunk with wine, wherein is excess; but be filled with the Spirit"? Jesus is the living Word of God (Revelation 19:13). Since the Bible is also the written Word of God, anything written in the Bible is the instruction of Jesus. Examine 2 Peter 3:9 to discover that the Lord "is not willing that any perish, but that all should come to repentance." Drunkenness is a soul-damning sin according to 1 Corinthians 6:10 which clearly states "drunkards" shall not inherit the kingdom of God. Therefore, making alcoholic wine at Cana would put Jesus at odds with His own intent of ministry (saving souls) and in conflict with His own Word.

Most of the crowd that wants Jesus to support social drinking would never allow Him to support drunkenness. But you can't have it only one way in this passage. Note that John 2:10 says that the governor of the feast indicated that the crowd had "well drunk" by the time Jesus made His wine. If what they had "well drunk" was intoxicating wine then Jesus was only adding to their drunkenness by making an extra 180 gallons of alcohol for the boozing crowd. If Jesus attended the wedding He was approving the wedding. If He saw the crowd of social drinkers already drunk, did not leave the function, but instead made more alcoholic wine,

He was approving their drunkenness. He would have never done that because of the grievous violation such action would pose to His own Word. In other words, He would have been the biggest hypocrite there.

Furthermore, if Jesus made alcoholic wine at Cana He was violating Habakkuk 2:15 which says, "Woe unto him that giveth his neighbour drink, that puttest thy bottle to him, and makest him drunken also, that thou mayest look on their nakedness!" He would have also violated Proverbs 23:29 which gives another curse, "Who hath woe? who hath sorrow? who hath contentions? who hath babbling? who hath wounds without cause? who hath redness of eyes?" How could Jesus do that to people? He wouldn't! At this point only the blind and the stubborn would fail to see Jesus Christ did not make alcoholic wine and was not giving His approval to social drinking. Would it not be ridiculously idiotic to claim Jesus provided the hard drug alcohol for men? Just because it is called wine in the passage does not in any fashion prove that it was an intoxicating drink. The word for wine used in this text is *oinos* which finds its meaning in the context. The context is Jesus Christ who cannot sin. This *oinos* has to be unfermented. It is the wine that comes from juice fresh squeezed from the grape (see Proverbs 3:10 and Isaiah 65:8)

Fact #2: If Jesus made intoxicating wine at Cana it would make Him just "one of the boys."

Jesus was and will never be "one of the boys." He will never party when it is time to party, sin when everybody is doing it and society has approved it, nor go along with the crowd to do evil so that He can fit in (see Exodus 23:2). On the contrary, Hebrews 4:15 states, "For we have not an high priest which cannot be touched with the feeling of our infirmities; but was in all points tempted like as we are, yet without sin." If Jesus Christ made alcohol at Cana He forfeited any possibility to save the world from their sin because He would have been participating in and/or applauding the sin of drunkenness (See 2 John 1:11). A sinner cannot save anyone. Jesus was the unblemished Lamb who took the sins of the world on Him at Calvary's Cross and suffered great agony to redeem us. He would have never blown His supreme mission with this one act at Cana. How can the Son of God come to take away sin and contribute to sin by making alcohol? That is impossible.

How would this have blown the mission? How would this have caused Him to be a sinner if He made alcoholic wine? Very simple: since Ephesians 5:18 commands us "be not drunk with wine," we have to examine what it means, in that passage, to be drunk. W. E. Vine, in his *Expositiory Dictionary of Old and New Testament Words* cites the Greek word for "drunk," *methusko*, as meaning, "to make drunk, or to grow drunk (an inceptive verb, marking the process of the state expressed, to become intoxicated)."[22] An inceptive verb in Greek, the New Testament original language, shows the process of beginning or becoming. Therefore, Ephesians 5:18 forbids not only the climaxing state of drunkenness from drinking an intoxicating beverage, it also forbids the process of becoming drunk.

Scripture commands you and I to abstain from anything that has the capacity to begin a process of becoming intoxicated. This rules out all drinking of intoxicating beverages. If Jesus made alcohol at Cana He would have violated Ephesians 5:18 by providing a substance that could make somebody drunk. The governor of the feast said they were "well drunk." This statement can mean either they were intoxicated or "had drank themselves to fullness." The latter meaning makes no sense. If they were full, why would they need anymore to drink. Be that as it may, the interpretation has no bearing upon the conclusion for Jesus' actions. To make Jesus a fermented wine-maker would make Him "one of the boys" who contributed to the sinfulness of the party. There is no doubt that 180 gallons of alcoholic wine could make the whole crowd drunk. That is what a lot of people want to do with Jesus - pull Him down to man's level. When you do that you make Him a sinner and you take away your possibility to be saved. By the way, you've got to stop ALL your social drinking if you want to obey Ephesians 5:18.

Fact #3: If Jesus Christ made intoxicating wine at Cana He "associated with evil."

1 Thessalonians 5:22 tells us to "abstain from all appearance of evil." Everybody knows that intoxicating beverages in today's culture, when it

---

[22]W. E. Vine, *Expository Dictionary of Old and New Testament Words* (Old Tappan: Fleming H. Revell, 1981), 341.

relates to personal conscience, are associated with evil. Furthermore, there is not one passage in all the Word of God which puts a good light upon drinking wine and strong drink for pleasure. Getting drunk today is associated with dark bars where they have turned the lights nearly off while men sin in dimly lit and smoke-filled rooms, relaxation after a hard day of work, chilling during vacation, and enjoying a glass of wine over dinner. John 3:19 says, "men loved darkness rather than light, because their deeds were evil."

Alcohol is associated with road fatalities, rapes, murders, broken homes, poverty, and divorces. It brings misery to those who are addicted to it and those who have to live with it in their families. "Abstain" means to "hold one's self from." Why would you want to have anything to do with alcohol if you're a Christian? Jesus didn't have anything to do with it. He DID NOT make alcoholic wine because that would have associated Himself with evil. He of all people would have been careful not to do that. Though the Bible says He was a friend of "publicans and sinners," He didn't make the drink or the drinker drink alcohol. His only association with sinners who drank was for the mission, to rescue them from their plight. His morals were not tainted. His motives were not mixed. His intent was never clouded. His message was never contradictory.

Fact #4: If Jesus made intoxicating wine at Cana He destroyed His influence for good.

How could this Jesus who preached in the Sermon on the Mount that His disciples were to be the "salt of the earth" and the "light of the world" serve alcohol to the wedding participants and His own disciples? It is ridiculous to believe such. As mentioned in our discussion of Fact #2, men's minds are warped to make Him a promoter of corruption in the midst of a holy ministry. John 2:11 says, "This beginning of miracles did Jesus in Cana of Galilee, and manifested forth his glory; and his disciples believed on him." There would have been no glory in six pots full of booze. This very verse would never have been written had Jesus made alcohol. His disciples could have no trust in Him if He turned water into an intoxicating beverage for the crowd to get more drunk. That is, Jesus would have hurt His reputation, and therefore His ability to influence people towards good, if He had made alcohol.

Even today, in modern culture, people are "turned off" if they see a Christian sipping their margaritas in a restaurant. From my experience, the critics of Christianity are looking for a loophole to excuse their sin. Seeing a boozing Christian provides one. They are disgusted at the scene, ready to denounce the hypocritical "Christian" for telling them to stop sinning and get saved, when that "Christian" has no more regard for righteousness than they do. You don't want to be accused of Romans 2:24: "the name of God is blasphemed among the Gentiles through you."

The very idea that Jesus Christ, the Son of the Living Righteous God, would serve 180 gallons of mind-numbing, testimony-destroying, sin-serving cordials is scandalous and blasphemous. God brands the sense of what is right upon the conscience of unbeliever and believer alike. Everyone knows when they are doing wrong unless their conscience is "seared with a hot iron" because they have sent the Holy Spirit away by their constant rebellion. The Church is losing her influence upon a godless world by drinking the devil's brew. Jesus had no part with that! Neither should you!

Fact #5: If Jesus made intoxicating wine at Cana He would have cast doubt upon His deity.

As will be seen in the next stated fact, the miracle of Cana was all about proving Jesus' deity. He would have never done anything that would cast doubt upon His membership in the Godhead. There are seven miracles in John's Gospel and all of them graphically illustrate Christ's deity. This one shows that Jesus Christ is the Creator, alongside God the Father. Speaking of Jesus the Creator, Paul writes in Colossians 1:16, "For by him were all things created, that are in heaven, and that are in earth, visible and invisible, whether they be thrones, or dominions, or principalities, or powers: all things were created by him, and for him." So, what Jesus created at the wedding of Cana was to prove His deity and bring Him glory. Which better aligns Jesus with the original creation by God the Father: fermented or unfermented wine?

The fact is that nowhere in the natural creation will you find alcoholic wine. As we discussed in Chapter One, modern day wines are an invention of man, the result of processes imposed upon the sweet grape juice that causes it to ferment. Yeast and heat are required to interfere with the natural process to turn sweet juice into sour, intoxicating wine. The only thing that can be made without these two artificial influences, heat and yeast, is a fruit vinegar. Grape juice will not turn alcoholic on its own. It will turn bitter like vinegar.

There is much evidence today that man has corrupted the natural and supernatural creative work of God. If Jesus had made fermented wine, He would have been aligning Himself with man's corruption of the original creation, taking the goodness of the grape and defiling it. Furthermore, yeast was considered an unholy substance to the Jews. On Passover, the holiest feast observed among the Jews which commemorates their deliverance from Egypt by the blood of an unblemished lamb, the father of the home instructed his whole family to search their house meticulously and remove any leaven from the premises (See Exodus 12:15). Jesus used leaven as a metaphor to speak of the evil teachings of the Pharisees (Matthew 16:6). If Jesus had naturally or supernaturally created intoxicating wine at Cana by miraculous intervention the people would have believed this act involved something unholy. The witnesses of this miracle verified that the process which took months to harvest grapes, squeeze them in the winepress to extract the juice, and store this juice in air tight containers only took Jesus a few minutes to accomplish. That's all that was needed to recognize a miracle. By the laws of nature, which Christ ordained in Creation, raindrops would fall from heaven, enter the ground, proceed up the capillaries of the vine, and become juicy grapes. Why would Christ ruin it all by going overboard with an alcoholic concoction? He wouldn't! He started with water and gave them grape juice, which the Bible also calls "wine."

Augustine, the fifth century Christian theologian, rightly observed, "For he on that marriage-day made wine in the six jars which he ordered to be filled with water, he who now makes it every year in the vines; for, as what the servants had poured into the water- jars was turned into wine by the power of the Lord, so, also, that which the clouds pour forth is turned into wine by the power of the self-same Lord."[23] Augustine was referring

---

[23] William Patton, *Bible Wines or the Laws of Fermentation and Wines of the Ancients* (New York: National Temperance Society and Publication House, 1874), 91.

to non-alcoholic grapes on the vine which are produced and watered by the Lord of creation. The Bible student will acknowledge that Isaiah 65:8 indicates even the cluster of grapes was called "new wine." Jesus' deed counts as a miracle not because of what He made but because of how quickly He made it. The miracle of Cana was one of time, not content. The Lord of time, who dwelleth in eternity, had supernatural powers to produce in a moment a product that brought Him glory and no harm to man. Anything more than that is the figment of an imagination that runs contrary to the witness of Scripture.

Fact #6: If Jesus made intoxicating wine at Cana, then the assessment by the ruler of the feast makes no sense.

Hear the verses again: "When the ruler of the feast had tasted the water that was made wine, and knew not whence it was: (but the servants which drew the water knew;) the governor of the feast called the bridegroom, And saith unto him, Every man at the beginning doth set forth good wine; and when men have well drunk, then that which is worse: but thou hast kept the good wine until now." Why would the governor of the feast declare it "good wine" if it was alcoholic? That may be the definition of today's modern wine which looks for five characteristics: sweetness (sugar content), acidity (the tingling taste which is really the alcohol content), astringent quality (comes from the tannins in the wine caused by skins and seeds, bitter and drying to the mouth), fruity taste (identifying the fruit used), and full-bodied (having higher alcohol content causing it to bead on the side of the glass). None of that applied to "good wine" in Bible days. The quality test went in the opposite direction. Good wine was sweet. It was a staple drink of ancient Israel. Fresh wine, fresh squeezed grape juice, a sweet drink was their goal.

Jesus himself spoke of the foolishness of putting "new wine" into "old wineskins." This practice rather quickly spoke of the action which new wine would do to an old wineskin. In the Bible, a wineskin was literally that - an animal skin that had been scraped, fully tanned and sewn together as a bottle to hold the grape juice. Old wineskins were progressively losing their elasticity. Stored grape juice by nature would produce gasses that swelled the wineskin. New wine in old wineskins would burst the stitching of the wineskin and they would lose their product. This explanation is in no way to attempt a denial that there was intoxicating wine in Bible days, nor claim that people did not get drunk. Chapter Two calls attention to Noah and Lot getting drunk. But to get drunk they had to have imbibed new wine that had gone sour, fermented, and was intoxicating. This is not at all a biased extrapolation when you read Psalm 104:14-15, "He causeth the grass to grow for the cattle, and herb for the service of man: that he may bring forth food out of the earth; And wine that maketh glad the heart of man, and oil to make his face to shine, and bread which strengtheneth man's heart." Though the Hebrew *yayin* is used in the Psalmist's declaration the lexicon and the context supports fresh wine from the vineyard. It came from the earth. The wine here is indicating new grape juice. Jesus' intent in the miracle was to make the heart glad, not drunk. Most drinkers are not always glad. Sometimes they're obnoxious, hateful, fighting, abusive, and crude in their behavior.

The most obvious way to discern what kind of wine the governor spoke of in Jesus' miracle is to pay special attention to his statement. He said that at most weddings of that day they brought out the good wine first and lastly the wine that is worse. But he said that Jesus served the "good wine," obviously the best wine, last. The worst wine in that day would be the soured wine, the aged wine, the fermented alcoholic concoction that was bitter and biting to the tongue. The best wine, good wine would be the fresh wine, sweet with no alcohol. If the attendees to the Cana wedding were "well drunk," that is intoxicated as the text indicates, the governor had already gotten to his worst wine. They had consumed all the sweet grape juice and then had to be served the old wine which had fermented. They were out of wine, both good and bad. It could not be the other way around given the culture and the mindset.

At Pentecost the disciples were perceived to be drunk as evidenced by the comment of the critics, "these men are full of new wine." Now, the comment came from "mockers," so you cannot pay much attention to their reasoning, since new wine is grape juice (see the discussion of *tiyrowsh* in Chapter One). But you can pay avid attention to Peter's explanation which is of utmost importance. He said, "these men are not drunk," because they are full of the Spirit. New wine will do that for you: make you glad. Worse wine, sour wine, fermented wine will make you drunk, often eliciting unseemly behavior. New wine will never make you drunk because it is not an intoxicant. The governor of the Cana feast was amazed that instead of serving alcohol, Jesus served new wine, grape juice, indicating the preferred choice of the two. It demonstrated an affirmation that these social occasions favored sobriety over intoxication. I'm sure, if you're honest, you now feel the same as the governor in Cana for learning the truth about this miracle. Or maybe you're angry that you can't keep blaming Jesus for your sin of drinking.

Warren Wiersbe stated, "Wine was the normal drink of the people in that day, and we must not use this miracle as an argument for the use of alcoholic beverages today."[24] Check any Bible Dictionary and you will discover that the wines of Jesus' day were diluted three to four parts of water to one part grape juice.[25] In some cases, the juice of the grape that had entered the fermentation stage was diluted as much as twenty times with water. Robert Stein confirmed this fact:

> Drinking wine unmixed....was looked upon as a 'Scythian' or barbarian custom. Why? In Biblical times the wine that was commonly used was diluted with water at the normal ratio of three parts water to one part wine. This means modern alcoholic beverages frequently possess alcoholic content three to ten times greater than wines of antiquity. Accordingly one would have to drink over twenty-two glasses...to consume the amount of alcohol that is in two martinis.[26]

This would not in any wise compare to the modern day counterpart called wine. The alcoholic content was just not there in Bible days until it was modified by human intervention and artificial fermenting processes. These same sources will also indicate that the grape juice was boiled and reduced to a sweet syrup whereby it could be kept without the possibility

---

[24] Warren W. Wiersbe, *Be Alive* (Wheaton: Scripture Press Publications, 1986), 28.

[25] J. D. Davis, *Davis Dictionary of the Bible* (Grand Rapids: Baker Book House, 1924), 868.

[26] Robert Stein, "Wine Drinking in New Testament Times." *Christianity Today*, June 20, 1975, 9-11.

of fermentation. Smith's Bible Dictionary quoted Canon Farrar on Bible wines:

> The simple wines of antiquity were incomparably less deadly than the stupefying and ardent beverages of our western nations. The wines of antiquity were more like sirups; many of them were not intoxicant; many more intoxicant in a small degree; and all of them, as a rule, taken only when largely diluted with water. They contained, even undiluted, but 4 or 5 percent of alcohol.[27]

The dilution factor indicates what the Jews considered to be "good wine." It was not intoxication that appealed to them, else they would not have diluted the wine. It was the sweet juice of the grape that appealed to their tastes as a daily drink.

Now, one more discovery is needed to establish the essence of the governor's statement. The unquestionable truth lies in the language. It usually does. The governor declared that Jesus made "good wine." There are two words for "good" in the New Testament language: *agathos* and *kalos*. You might think that the first word would be used in this text, *agathos*, speaking of something simply good, good in its character. *Agathos* is the chief word used in the New Testament to speak of God's goodness. It is used in Matthew 19:17 when Jesus spoke to the rich young ruler and said, "there is none good but one, that is, God." It is the Bible's word for speaking of something Christians should "cleave to" (Romans 12:9). *Agathos* is the word of the New Testament to speak of something that is of a good nature, useful, pleasant, agreeable, something that makes a person happy and joyful.

The other word, *kalos*, distinguishes something that is morally good, pure, and praiseworthy for its honorable value and virtue. When the woman with the alabaster box, in Matthew 26, broke the box to anoint Jesus' feet, He said of her that "she hath wrought a good work upon me."

---

[27]Dr. William Smith, "Wine," *Smith's Bible Dictionary*, 1901, https://www.biblestudytools.com/dictionaries/smiths-bible-dictionary/wine.html.

He was indicating that her action of anointing him with the precious and expensive oil was morally pure, a sacrificial act. He was contrasting her heart with those who resented the ointment being wasted. Jesus knew that in their hearts they could not stand to see a profit forfeited for such a lavish expression of worship. Her act was praiseworthy because it was honorable in value and virtue.

While I was writing this chapter I called my faithful friend to discuss my findings in the John 2 Cana miracle. I mentioned the governor's comment about saving the "good" wine for last. I asked him, "of the two words for good in the Greek New Testament, *agathos* and *kalos*, which one would you guess to be used in John 2"? He quickly replied *agathos*, which had been my guess also. It means good in its character. I said, "No, it is *kalos*," and he shouted with glee over the phone saying, "then it was wine that was morally pure, perfectly pure." The governor's words give it away. The wine Jesus made at Cana was intrinsically pure in all its qualities making it a moral beverage to drink. As you can see, Jesus did not make alcoholic wine at Cana.

Interestingly enough, the word *agathos* would not have been the best word to use if this wine Jesus made was alcoholic. To help clarify, examine where the two words appear together in Scripture. Both words appear in Romans 7:18 where Paul said, "For I know that in me (that is, in my flesh,) dwelleth no good thing." Paul testified that in his flesh, which is our carnal nature, which desires to follow the path of sin over righteousness, there is no *agathos* thing. *Agathos* is the quality of being beneficial in its affect. Alcohol is never beneficial in its affect. It kills brains cells. It cripples the liver. It drags the victim into wrong thinking and wrong living. Yet, Paul went on to say, "for to will is present with me; but how to perform that which is good I find not." Paul said in his flesh he had a will to choose *kalos*, morally good and righteous behavior, but he often could not find the performance of this noble and God-honoring behavior since the flesh was more powerfully winning over his choices. He was blocked in his pure behavior because it was not intrinsically within him. The wine that Jesus made that day was *kalos*. It was good within itself. *Kalos* means "perfectly pure" and "intrinsically good," so how could it have been alcoholic? It could not! No one should say it was and lie against the testimony of the governor and the accuracy of the text.

There is one thing for sure. Bible novices would seek to use Jesus to justify moderate or social drinking by this miracle in Cana. However, they must know that Jesus was a teetotaler while on the earth and unquestionably a teetotaler in Heaven. He said in Matthew 26:29, "But I say unto you, I will not drink henceforth of this fruit of the vine, until that day when I drink it new with you in my Father's kingdom." He has not even let the first sip come to His lips since He left this earth, grape juice or alcoholic wine. That is the truth! For every advocate of moderate, social drinking, making Jesus the justifier of such sinfulness, there is a quotable Bible scholar who will not let truth fall in the streets and point out the fallacy of believing such defilement of the Saviour's character. To associate Christ with the approval of drinking alcohol is Biblically irrational and spiritually insane.

Chapter Nine

"Not Given to Much Wine"

The phrase, "not given to much wine," has caused more misunderstanding concerning the Christian's stance on drinking alcohol beverages than perhaps any other passage of Scripture. Misunderstanding Scripture always leads to confusion about what is righteous and what is unrighteous. May I just use one of Paul's favorite phrases on the matter: "Brethren, I would not have you to be ignorant." For the moderate drinker there is a tendency to camp out on the word "much." To camp out on an adjective and ignore the meaning of the prohibition is the height of ignorant usage of the Word of God. In this text you should concentrate on the "not given" more than the "much" if you ever expect to understand Paul's meaning. Making this passage an artificial and false loophole in the warning of God about alcohol is spiritually dangerous.

The phrase is given in two places of God's word: 1 Timothy 3:8 and Titus 2:3. The first appearance of the phrase addresses deacons. "Likewise must the deacons be grave, not doubletongued, **not given to much wine**, not greedy of filthy lucre." The second admonishes "aged women," "that they be in behaviour as becometh holiness, not false accusers, **not given to much wine**, teachers of good things." Upon general observation of this passage would it not be absolutely mind boggling that any aged woman would make this passage in Titus to be a permission for drinking in moderation? How could that be? Whatever the phrase means in Titus must be consistent with Timothy's instructions that the women exhibit "behavior as becometh holiness" and "teachers of good things." Would the winebibbing woman or even the casual drinker dare to think she can drink alcohol and show holiness or teach good things to others? Such is a double lifestyle, one of pure hypocrisy. Now, we want to examine the phrase fully to see if we can find the least endorsement by God that either party, deacons or aged women, can drink alcohol. It is impossible to find such duplicitous instruction in the text.

First of all, let us recognize that by logical comparison these verses cannot for a moment put God's approval on drinking a "little" alcohol. If the prohibition concentrates on the word "much" to justify a "little" alcohol the interpreter becomes foolish in their understanding. When Solomon says in Ecclesiastes 7:17, "be not over much wicked...why shouldest thou die before thy time," are we to assume that the wisest man in the Bible meant that we could be moderately wicked, a little wicked, every now and then wicked so that we could die when we're supposed to die? Is that not the most foolish reasoning? And yet, it is exactly the same reasoning that turns Titus 2:3 and 1 Timothy 3:8 into a loophole for a little liquor? When Paul wrote, "And do not be conformed to this world," does that mean a little worldliness is acceptable? The emphasis is not on "much" to justify a little.

Again 1 Peter 4:4 speaks of Christians who've forsaken the lifestyle of the Gentiles (a word literally translated heathen), and the world speaks evil of them because they no longer run with the crowd that participates in lasciviousness, lusts, excess of wine, revellings, banquetings, abominable idolatries, and excess of rioting. Rioting, in that text, speaks of being a prodigal, abandoning God and living a loose, sinful life. Would we assume for a moment that Peter would be permitting a "little rioting," drinking a "little wine" with the heathen, being a "part-time" prodigal, moderately loose at times before God? The provocative point is that the language that condemns excessive indulgence in no way implies the action is permissible in smaller amounts. Such thinking is wicked and woefully ignorant!

In case you are not convinced, let's do a few more substitutions into the phrase. For instance, since we know that alcohol kills brain cells, would we override the prohibition here if it had read, "not given to much cocaine." Cocaine causes permanent damage to the blood vessels in the heart and brain. So does alcohol. Cocaine is a hard drug. So is alcohol. How about "not given to much poison"? Would that mean a little cyanide would be alright for the Christian who deliberately ignores the warning? Do not consider my reasoning preposterous.

Surely by now you recognize that we cannot interpret "much" to endorse a little moderate drinking of alcohol. Not only is the reasoning unjustified, but it is also inconsistent with Biblical understanding. The apostle Paul reasoned with the Galatians when he said, "Are ye so foolish? having begun in the Spirit, are ye now made perfect by the flesh?" (Galatians 3:3) Paul was questioning the sanity of the Galatians who were going backward in the basis of their salvation faith to arrive at perfection through the flesh. Be careful social drinker, moderate drinker, casual drinker! You should not go backwards to the things salvation delivered you from. 1 Corinthians 6:11 says, "such were some of you: but ye are washed, but ye are sanctified." How can the Christian go backwards from the washing? Is it all right to go back to a little sinning? If you can make "not given to much wine" a permission for alcoholic wine in moderation, you had better check to see if you've ever been washed or sanctified in the blood of Jesus Christ. Are you truly saved?

Going a little further, we can expand the original two occurrences (1 Timothy 3:8 and Titus 2:3) to five occurrences in Scripture. In 1 Timothy 3:3, we read that the bishop is to be, "not given to wine." Without the defining adjective "much," the Greek text renders this prohibition *me paraoinos* as "not even alongside or around wine." The word "vigilant" in verse 2 is specifically used to express "abstaining from wine." The Greek word for vigilant, *nephalios*, in general, speaks of being temperate or sober. This bishop or elder, then must be sober-minded. You cannot do that when you "sit long at the wine." Bishops/pastors must abstain.

Then 1 Timothy 3:8, as previously discussed, says the deacons are "not given to much wine." The Greek reads *me prosecho polus oinos* is translated in the New American Standard Bible, "not addicted to much wine." The warrant for this translation is in the word *prosecho* which describes a person who attaches themselves to wine and it has a hold on them. I dare anybody to refute the meaning of this text. It warns specifically not to even be around the intoxicant for fear of its addictive character.

The third occurrence is 1 Timothy 3:11 which addresses the wives of deacons, calling them to abstain. *Nephalios* is the word used in this text and also used in Titus 2:2. Abstinence is heralded in both passages. The fourth occasion, Titus 2:2, addresses the "aged men" calling them to be sober and temperate - *nephalios* (abstain) and *sophron* (self-controlled and curbing one's desires and impulses). This too would forbid the usage of anything that controlled the mind or hindered sober thinking. There is no distinction of permission for drinking alcohol between deacons and aged men.

Finally, the "aged women" are told in Titus 2:3 to be "not given to much wine," the same phrase with one word change - *me douloo polus oinos*. If you are familiar with Greek you may immediately recognize *douloo* as referring to a servant. The intent of the meaning goes quite farther and speaks of any substance, including wine, that brings the person into slavery and bondage.

The vast majority of alcohol drinkers are in great denial claiming that the inebriating drink never brings them into captivity or bondage. However, anyone who puts an intoxicating liquid to their lips has invited intoxication into the mind and the body. The first drink technically and spiritually and physically ends a sober condition (we will discuss this in detail in Chapter Twelve).

Now, as you examine these injunctions for the preservation of the witness of pastors, deacons, deacon's wives, and aged saints, anyone who reads into the Scripture a "private interpretation" that some cannot drink at all and some can drink a little makes God a "respecter of persons," which Acts 10:34 categorically denies. We do not serve a God of double-standards. He is a God who raises higher standards for spiritual leaders but that is a horse of a different color. He is not a God of double-standards that would have one set of moral principles for Christians in the south and another for Christians in the north. He does not permit one to drink moderately and commanding others to abstain. Such thinking is preposterous. As witnessed in the literal translations of these five passages, there is a call for strict abstinence from alcohol in any form that hinders or kills sobriety in the Christian. The obvious reason in all five cases is for the preservation of a testimony of holiness.

There is a final observation in the passages that may be overlooked. A good Bible student notices the peripheral wording as well as the primary wording. Twice in Timothy and twice in Titus (if you include the instruction to young men in verse 6) there is the special word *hosautos* which is translated three times as "likewise" and once, for the deacon's wives, "even so." The word is deliberate. Translated, it means "in like manner" or in the "same way." The intentional framework for these texts is to show there is no difference of consideration in the mandates for all five people. All of them are to conduct their lifestyle in the same way. All are to be honorable. All are to be holy. All are to be temperate in the same way. All are to be sober. All are prescribed a prohibition from wine. All of them are to abstain from the alcoholic beverage. It is in no way a reference to grape juice with no alcoholic content, as some have surmised, else there would be no prohibition except for gluttony. Such would make no sense. It is a prohibition from alcohol. That is God's truth for those who will rightly divide the Word and for those who will heed the Word.

In conclusion let us hear from the Bible the greatest quote from the greatest abstainer from alcohol. "And they gave him to drink wine mingled with myrrh: but he received it not." The preeminent Christian leader, the founder of Christianity, the only true Sovereign in the Universe, Jesus Christ, when He was offered wine in a time it was perhaps most needed, He refused it. If that action was good for Jesus it is most certainly good for us all. Surely someone there at the crucifixion may have said, "it's okay to have a little," but He said NO! Be ye imitators of God as dear children (Ephesians 5:1).

Chapter Ten

The Double Portrait of Wine

When you understand that not everything that is called wine in the Bible is the equivalent of our modern day wines, a double portrait begins to come into focus. The defining rule is that the context of the passage determines whether the wine referenced was fermented or unfermented. *Yayin* is not always fermented wine, though the bulk of the Scripture using this word denotes fermented wine. *Oinos* is not always fermented wine either, since the parable of wine bottles speaks of *neos oinos* (new wine and therefore grape juice) put into old wine bottles. For reference, a wine bottle in Bible days was the hind leg of a lamb skin, tanned, and sewn together to make a container. There is no doubt that this parable refers to fresh grape juice that will emit gasses in a confined container and burst the seams of an old wineskin. Thus the context determines the usage.

With two types of wine, fermented/diluted and unfermented, two symbolic portraits appear in the Scriptures concerning God's dealings with mankind. One portrait is of blessing. The other portrait is of judgment and punishment. There is no confusion when we find Genesis 27:28 speaking positively about wine, "Therefore God give thee of the dew of heaven, and the fatness of the earth, and plenty of corn and wine." The word used is *tiyrowsh*, which with few exceptions speaks of fresh juice from the grape. Yet, when *yayin* is used, the normal word for fermented wine, and God speaks of it in rewarding terms, we are caught in the web of confusion and struggle to determine the truth about drinking alcohol. The struggle disappears, however, when we consider the context. I will state it again. *Yayin* is a generic term for wine, but almost always refers to fermented wine. *Tiyrowsh* is a specific term, and with few exceptions indicates unfermented wine - grape juice. Yet, *Tiyrowsh* is never used as a portrait of God's judgment.

How is it that the same God who says, "wine is a mocker and strong drink is raging," would declare in Psalm 104:15 that He gives the "wine that maketh glad the heart of man, and oil to make his face to shine, and bread which strengtheneth man's heart"? Why is this *yayin* in Psalm 104:15 instead of *tiyrowsh* if God is opposed to alcohol consumption? If you believe God's word is without error and the character of God never changes (see Hebrews 13:8) there can be only one answer. *Yayin* in Psalm 104:15, considered in context, must not be fermented or it must be diluted syrup of the grapes boiled down to minimal or no alcoholic content. This is not conjecture. It is solid Bible interpretation established by context and historical/cultural facts (See Chapter Eleven).

God blesses man with good things. James 1:17 says, "Every good gift and every perfect gift is from above, and cometh down from the Father of lights, with whom is no variableness, neither shadow of turning." 1 Timothy 6:17 says God gives us "richly all things to enjoy." Yet, we must keep in mind that man does not enjoy alcohol. Alcohol enjoys man, engulfs man, deceives man, and enslaves man. There is no justification in crediting God for alcohol when in fact He gave us the good gift of grape juice. It is man that corrupts the good gift and makes alcohol.

In stark contrast to the picture of wine (*tiyrowsh* grape juice) being a blessing to man from God, there is a portrait of wine in the Bible that is symbolic of God's punitive judgment on man. Psalm 60:3 says, "Thou hast shewed thy people hard things: thou hast made us to drink the wine of astonishment." David speaks in this passage of God allowing enemies to prevail over us because He is displeased with us. In this case man is, metaphorically speaking, forced by God to drink of the wine of *tar'elah*, a word that means reeling, staggering, or trembling. It is a fitting image, that of a drunkard staggering. There is no doubt that *yayin* in this text is the fermented drink. God can knock us off our feet, cause us to tremble and stagger, under the swift hand of His judgment, when our life has become a displeasure to His heart.

Perhaps the most prominent and frightening passage where God uses wine as the image of judgment is Revelation 14 where Babylon, the end-times empire of spiritual fornication, will fall and "drink of the wine of the wrath of God, which is poured out without mixture into the cup of his indignation." This is a familiar reference to all first century recipients who knew of the "mixing bowl," commonly called a *krater*, wherein wine was diluted with water to minimize the alcoholic content. John's revelation is that all those people and nations who are aligning themselves with the Antichrist, and rebelling against Almighty God will drink of God's undiluted wrath. This is wrath of full force.

Jeremiah wrote of the original Babylon which corrupted God's people through idolatry and animalistic sin: "Babylon hath been a golden cup in the LORD'S hand, that made all the earth drunken: the nations have drunken of her wine; therefore the nations are mad" (Jeremiah 51:7). The description is fitting because Babylon has always represented idolatry, which is turning away from God to other competing affections. Men try to celebrate their sin during respectable events - weddings, parties, social gatherings, business meetings - but God sees through it all. Divine judgment has no mixture and exposes the sinner with full wrath, a rude awakening for the hardened sinner who rejects God's counsel.

There is a powerful motive behind God's message declaring the double-portrait of wine in the sacred text. We should ask, "How can God favor the consumption of fermented wine, much less strong drink, when He uses such a substance as the image of promised, devastating judgment upon the rebellious hearts of this world"? Is He a doting God who simply turns His head the other way when men engage in revelry, drunkenness, intoxication to any degree, or social drinking under the guise of social conformity? If drinking alcohol is permissible with God in moderation are all the other sins permissible with God in moderation? The portrait of judgment answers these questions with a resounding warning that all men must take heed: judgment is coming on all those who rebel against God's truth.

I had a neighbor who just couldn't leave the liquor bottle alone. His work called and asked if I knew of his whereabouts. I did not know where he was but decided to check his mobile home. As I pulled up, his car was in the driveway. That was a good indication that the poor man was home laying out of work. I knocked on the door three times and with no answer decided to see if the door was unlocked. It was and I proceeded to enter the residence. I found this man, whom I loved deeply and pastorally, laid out unconscious on his bed with an opened, empty bottle of pills on the nightstand. There were three or four pills on the carpet. Fortunately, a 911 call and subsequent trip to the hospital to pump his stomach saved the man's life. His estranged wife, who dearly adored him but could not tolerate his drunken sprees, decided to take him back into her home for watchcare.

Two years later, his sons came to my house and asked me again if I knew where their daddy might be. I told them I did not but that I would go and ask God to find him. There in my study I knelt in prayer and God answered my prayer. Hearing this might lead you to suspect I had some kind of prior knowledge of the man's intent that day. I did not! I simply believed Jeremiah 33:3, "Call unto me, and I will answer thee, and shew thee great and mighty things, which thou knowest not," a promise that is crucial in times of crisis. God said, "Go up on the mountain and you will find him in his car attempting suicide again."

I told the boys and they immediately rushed up the mountain. There, on the side of the road, was this dear soul who couldn't stand his life. He had connected a hose pipe from the exhaust and inserted the other end in a barely cracked rear window. My friend and neighbor was already unconscious. We thought he was surely dead this time. However, he survived and started attending church quite regularly. Unfortunately he never seemed to get victory over his demons and his vice. Since leaving that pastorate I've often wondered what happened to him. God permitted me to rescue, love, and share the message of deliverance with him many times. I can only hope that his heart on some special day since I left, connected with the truth in Luke 4:18 that the Spirit of the Lord is upon Jesus and He came to "preach deliverance to the captive" and "set at liberty them that are bruised." Included with the promise of future judgment on the sinfully rebellious are those internal afflictions to the soul for those who do not take God seriously when He says, "Wine is a mocker."

Chapter Eleven

Is Unfermented Wine in Bible Days a Myth?

Since Chapter One gives a thoroughly documented word study of two types of wine in the Old Testament, and two types of wine in the New Testament based upon the contextual usage of *oinos,* it is hard to imagine anyone claiming that unfermented wine in Bible days is a myth. Yet, that is the clear assertion of Dr. Randy Jaeggli, Ph.D. professor at Bob Jones University. In his book, *Christians and Alcohol: A Scriptural Case for Abstinence*, Jaeggli violated his own clarion call for objective exegesis of the Scripture. He stated, "It is vitally important that we undertake our interpretive investigations with objectivity and let the Scripture dictate what we believe, rather than approaching the bible with a presupposition in mind that our investigation will by all means support."[28]

Yet, Jaeggli ignored clear passages in the Old Testament that definitively distinguish *yayin* as grape juice and *tiyrowsh* as the same. He also disregarded contextual identification of *oinos* as unfermented in some cases within the New Testament. Jaeggli stated categorically, "there is no Old Testament usage of *yayin* that demands the interpretive conclusion that it was grape juice," and "there is no use of *oinos* in the New Testament that requires the interpretive conclusion that it was unfermented grape juice."[29]

---

[28] Randy Jaeggli, *Christians and Alcohol: A Scriptural Case for Abstinence* (Greenville: Bob Jones University Press, 2014), 41.

[29] Ibid., 44 and 83.

What about Isaiah 65:8? Dr. Jaeggli calls for "special examination," yet his exegesis is more like "special evasion" of the glaring truth. Isaiah tells us that *tiyrowsh* is "found in the cluster." Jaeggli queries incredibly, "how is it that *tiros* can be found in a grape that has not even been crushed yet by treading?"[30] If the professor had reviewed his own material he would have remembered his answer to his own question. The "new wine," *tiyrowsh*, is found in the cluster when it is first draining from grapes or squeezed by the king's servant directly into a cup. Nehemiah was a cupbearer to king Artaxerxes and had done this many times. Would anybody of normal sense, much less skilled in proper exegesis, call this substance fermented wine?

Jaeggli practices the same kind of exegesis in the examination of Proverbs 3:10. He calls the "new wine," that comes forth from the presses, a fermented substance because yeast is present on the skin of the grape and fermentation begins immediately in the wine vat. Claiming such is an extreme stretch to the point of absurdity. His further assertion that wine fermentation is an anaerobic process and thereby unavoidably leads to alcoholic content ignores a crucial reality in wine making. The first stage of the process, collecting the juice which is an aerobic condition, meaning the juice requires certain amounts of oxygen to put the yeast into the reproductive phase, will either lead to success or failure. If there is not enough oxygenation for the yeast to reproduce, then the sugar cannot be converted to ethanol, and instead will convert to sour vinegar. All winemakers testify of the tenuous nature of the process which can ruin in the slightest failure of attaining proper conditions for fermentation. As noted, in that case, the grape juice turns to fruit vinegar. To claim that there is enough yeast present on the skin of the grape, before it is perforated, to make alcohol is a preposterous claim.

One more point of review of Jaeggli's book is warranted that no confusion results in the mind of unsuspecting readers. The professor criticizes "overly zealous proponents of the Temperance Movement," but is guilty of the same when he pits A. M. Wilson's, *The Wines of the Bible: An Examination and Refutation of the Unfermented Wine Theory* against William Patton's, *Bible Wines or the Laws of Fermentation and*

---

[30]Ibid., 67.

Wines of the Ancients. Jaeggli claims that Wilson "decimated" all of Patton's documentation for the ancient preservation of unfermented wine. Yet in his book, Jaeggli fails to demonstrate how Wilson disproves Patton's conclusions.

These two source books of the Temperance Movement were only published six years apart and are obviously written from opposing views. I have read Patton's book but I have not read Wilson's book. Comparing the superfluous quotes Jaeggli gave from Wilson's book with the material in Patton's book proves to my mind that Wilson's conclusions are woefully lacking. Jaeggli shows his bias when he says that it is unfortunate that Patton's book has been reprinted by Challenge Press. Such a statement reveals a loss of credibility as an author. Suppressing resources we disagree with is no valid way to ascertain truth. The only source of unquestionable truth is the Bible. Truth does not come by choosing sides with human interpreters. Truth comes by honest investigation of the full witness of Scripture on any subject allowing the Holy Spirit to be our Guide (see John 16:13).

Unfermented wine, diluted wine with meager alcoholic content, and preservation of sweet grape juice for long periods of time in Bible days is so well documented in multiple sources besides Patton's work, that only the naive or inept would assert otherwise. Aristotle, the Greek philosopher, who lived just after the close of the Old Testament, wrote, "sweet wine...does not inebriate as ordinary wine does." The same writes of his experience in 350 B.C. that "there is a kind of wine, for instance, which both solidifies and thickens by boiling - I mean, must." He is speaking of the boiled, fresh-squeezed juice of the grape that was called new wine.[31]

Hippocrates, a Greek physician living around 460-370 B.C., wrote of medicinal formulas he gave to his patients. One of those was boiled sweet wine which he still called wine after the boiling, although technically it was a sweet syrup. The doctor's testimony was "the sweet affects the

---

[31] Brumbelow, 72-74.

head less than the strong, attacks the brain less...."[32] Must, the thick syrup from boiling grape juice, would not inebriate and would affect the bladder more than the head.

Athenaeus, a Greek/Egyptian writer living during the 3rd century A.D., who compiled the oldest living cookbook of those times called *Deipnosophistae*, spoke of two different kinds of wine. Athenaeus referenced wine that was sweeter than honey and another kind of wine that was more bitter than nettles. Athenaeus refers to non-alcoholic and alcoholic wine respectively. If you doubt his conclusion, the following statement is unmistakable. "At the time of the festivals, he went about, and took wine (*oinos*) from the fields."[33] Only non-alcoholic wine comes from the fields.

Columella was a Roman living from 4 B.C. to about A.D. 70, which makes him a contemporary to Jesus Christ and the New Testament. This Roman writer recorded volumes on New Testament agriculture. Columella made a notable statement:

> Care should also be taken so that the must, when it has been pressed out, may last well or at any rate keep until it is sold. We will then next set forth how this ought to be brought about and by what preservatives the process should be aided. Some people put must in leaden vessels and by boiling reduce it by a quarter, others by a third. There is no doubt that anyone who boiled it down to one-half would be likely to make a better thick form of must and therefore more profitable for use, so much so that it can actually be used, instead of must boiled down to one-third, to preserve the must produced from old vineyards. We regard as the best wine any kind which can keep without any preservative, nor should anything at all be mixed with it by which its natural savour would be obscured; for that wine is most excellent which has given pleasure by its own

---

[32] Ibid., 75.

[33] Ibid., 78.

natural quality.[34]

Columella's statement proves that new wine called "must" was preserved by boiling it down to a third or even half of its volume. This reduction made it the "best wine" because it had no preservatives and no fermentation that spoiled its "natural" flavor.

Despite the evidence I just presented, please remember that it is not Aristotle's book, Hippocrates' book, Athenaeus' book, Columella's book, Patton's book, Wilson's book, or even this book that is the final authority. The final authority is God's book. The Bible clearly speaks of wine that comes directly from the agricultural field as noted in Isaac's blessing of Jacob. The patriarch asked for God to bless his son with the "dew of heaven, and the fatness of the earth, and plenty of corn and wine." This is *tiyrowsh*, not *yayin*.

In Genesis 27:25 God uses the word *yayin* to speak of the drink that Jacob, the deceiver, brought to his dad when he followed his mother's suggestion to serve fake venison made from goats. It was a hoax to steal the firstborn's blessing. How is it that God did not use *tiyrowsh* in both places in the story? The wine that Jacob brought to Isaac was *yayin*. It could have been fermented or not fermented. Many commentators believe it was fermented and propose that Isaac had a taste for the stuff. Maybe he did. Maybe he didn't. But given that Jacob took fermented wine to his dad, it most likely was provided to him by his mother who knew it would aid in the deception. But Isaac, even in a possible inebriated condition, could not speak a divine blessing which included fermented wine from the field. Corn does not come from the field fermented. The "fat of the earth" does not include fermentation. The language is clear because the intent is clear. The blessing is only on unfermented wine.

In Numbers 18:12, the priests in service at the Temple were to receive for their personal use "the best of the oil, and all the best of the wine, and of the wheat, the firstfruits of them which they shall offer unto the LORD." The best of the oil, wine and wheat were referred to by God as the "firstfruits." What are the firstfruits? This was the early part of the

---

[34]Ibid., 79.

harvest. It was not the oil that had matured, nor oil that had set on their shelves for years and become rancid. It was the freshest oil just pressed from the olives, offered to God in the purest and most desired form. This also included the fresh squeezed juice that was immediately brought to the Temple priests. It was not fermented. Fermentation, according to the Jews, began on the fifth day after pressing. The worshiper, giving of the firstfruits, may have even brought in grapes as well as grape juice since Isaiah 65:8 says the new wine (tiyrowsh) is "in the cluster."

Deuteronomy 11:14 says that God gives the "rain of your land in his due season, the first rain and the latter rain, that thou mayest gather in thy corn, and thy wine, and thine oil." Surely the simplest Bible student and the Bible professor both can see that given the other two fresh products of the harvest this is no reference to fermented wine. When there is an "agricultural mention" of corn, wine, or oil, the clear intention of the Biblical writer is to speak of a fresh, unfermented product.

In Joel 1:5 we encounter a new word for wine. "Awake, ye drunkards, and weep; and howl, all ye drinkers of wine, because of the new wine; for it is cut off from your mouth." The first word in the verse is *yayin* and the second word is the Hebrew word *aciyc*. Lexicons always indicate *aciyc* is "sweet wine pressed from juice." The verse makes perfect sense when you realize you can't get drunk without consuming a fermented beverage. You don't get a fermented beverage straight out of the field from fresh squeezed juice of the grape (*aciyc*). Two kinds of wine are in Joel 1:5 - fermented and unfermented. The latter is not a myth according to Scripture. No interpreter in their right mind can insist that *aciyc* refers to alcoholic wine. If they do they are proven wrong again when Joel 3:18 and Amos 9:13 indicate that the future kingdom of God will drip with *aciyc*. If someone thinks that God, in all He has said in the Biblical text to warn of the dangers of fermented drink, will have and approve of abundant supply of alcoholic drink in His future kingdom, that person is no doubt mindlessly drunk themselves! Believe God's Word for what it says and you will not go astray from the truth.

Carmen was our first convert in one small, shanty town just outside Lima, Peru. I began doing mission work in Peru, South America, in 1998 teaching missionaries about prayer. Walking in this vast sandy desert village outside of Lima, we encountered three women who were curious to why gringos were in their town. The marvelous result of that divine moment was that three ladies prayed to receive Christ as their Saviour. Carmen was especially friendly and had many questions. My missionary friend, Kevin Shearer, was my interpreter. Carmen asked him a question in Spanish and I was anxious to know what she was saying. When my friend Kevin looked at me and grinned with that characteristic grin of satisfaction I knew something was up. He said, "Tim, she's asked a question and I'm going to let you answer it." I agreed but when he told me what the question was I choked. She wanted to know whether it was right now to go to parties and drink alcohol like she did before she was saved. I breathed a desperate prayer in my spirit and said to her, "Carmen, whenever you are faced with that decision just pray to the God you have now in your heart and He'll tell you exactly what to do." I could have pointedly told her, "No, you cannot drink alcohol now." But I gave her the Spirit's counsel that soon would make the difference in her life.

On the day Dr. Shearer baptized Carmen, she told him, "I have to share my story with everyone present." She began, "I remember what the missionary said to me." That gripped Kevin's heart, wondering what she was going to say. Carmen continued, "He told me, 'Go ahead to the parties you like to attend, but before you take a drink, you ask God if it is okay for you to drink.'" Carmen then said that a month after she prayed to receive the Lord, she went to a party. The booze was flowing, as usually happens at these kinds of events. She grabbed a plastic cup of beer and started to take a drink. But Carmen remembered what pastor Tim told her. So, according to her testimony, Carmen prayed and asked, "Lord, is it okay for me to drink at these parties?" Carmen then said to the crowd at her baptism, "I lifted the cup to my lips and the beer tasted and smelled like sewage water to me. Then I knew that everything those men told me was true. I knew that Jesus was my Savior and Lord."

Carmen's life was changed completely leaving no place for alcohol ever again. She became part of a core group that helped launch a new church in the shanty town of Villa El Salvador (House of the Saviour). These are the eternal rewards of pastors and missionaries, seeing lives changed like Carmen's for the glory of God.

Chapter Twelve

Who Knows What Constitutes Drunkenness?

Unfortunately, many in the world and a few in the Church rely on their English classroom instruction to define drunkenness. Drink, Drank, Drunk: You're not drunk until you've passed the stages of "drink and drank." This is not how God defines drunkenness. Before the Biblical definition is given here, the matter of the consequences to drunkenness must be established. Most of the debate in Christian circles is about the quantity of alcohol consumed, not the shameful sin of drunkenness. Most Christians agree that drunkenness is a sin in God's eyes. It would be a shame not to believe this truth because God is explicit without question on the consequential damnation of drunkenness. Yet, if you do not know at what point you become drunk, you can never believe you've sinned in drunkenness.

You can recall from Chapter Eight how it was established that God is against the process of becoming drunk as well as the drunken state due to the inceptive verb of Ephesians 5:18. That means it is a sin in God's eyes for anyone to partake of an intoxicating drink just as much as it is a sin to become finally intoxicated. Our definition of sin comes from James 4:17: "Therefore to him that knoweth to do good, and doeth it not, to him it is sin." If a man or a woman takes a drink of a beer or wine and knows that God has said in His word that this is wrong, and does it anyway, THEY HAVE SINNED AGAINST GOD. If Ephesians 5:18 says it is wrong to even begin the process of intoxication, then drinking alcohol, especially for Christians, is sinful. Failure to acknowledge this truth places the disobedient heart in direct rebellion against God's Word.

We have learned from Proverbs 20 and 23 that drinking alcohol enslaves you. The description of an alcoholic drink in Proverbs 23 is noteworthy. It bubbles and turns or moves in the cup by itself. The deception factor of an alcoholic drink in Proverbs 20:1 is prohibitive. It makes a fool out of you. Every person who drinks alcohol is warned that the wine in the cup, the beer in the can, the liquor in the shot glass has the power to "bite" them with addiction like a coiled snake.

The worst consequence of drinking alcohol is the damnation of the soul. God will not be mocked. The drinker cannot somehow believe in his own mind that such lifestyle behavior will be excused at the Judgment Seat of God. 1 Corinthians 6:9-10 says, "Know ye not that the unrighteous shall not inherit the kingdom of God? Be not deceived: neither fornicators, nor idolaters, nor adulterers, nor effeminate, nor abusers of themselves with mankind, nor thieves, nor covetous, **nor drunkards**, nor revilers, nor extortioners, shall inherit the kingdom of God." Drunkards are included in the list with homosexuals, thieves, and fornicators. The drinker of alcohol, according to God, is no better than any one of the other nine given in the list. They all merit damnation in Hell as God sees it.

The self-righteous automatically and dangerously conclude the drunkard to be the staggering sot in society who has already pickled his liver and daily reeks of rotgut whiskey breath. It surely could not refer to the Christian who has an occasional beer or wine over dinner. What if God has another definition for drunkard than what we suppose? W. E. Vine indicated that the noun form (drunkard) marked "habitual intoxication."[35] Sometimes drunkenness and intoxication are two different things in our minds. In other words, you think someone can be intoxicated but not yet drunk. No such distinction appears in the Word of God. To be intoxicated is to be drunk and to be drunk is to be intoxicated by God's definition.

So you may ask: "Is it a little bit intoxicated or a lot intoxicated that constitutes drunkenness?" Again, to ask that question is to prove you missed God's point. God says it is a sin to be intoxicated or partaking of the intoxicating drink (See Ephesians 5:18 again). Furthermore, a person who makes it a habit of his or her life to believe and practice the

---

[35] Vine, 342.

consumption of alcohol faces damnation. A double life is not permitted in the Kingdom of God. 1 Corinthians, after listing those sins, continues in 6:11 with, "And such were some of you: but ye are washed, but ye are sanctified, but ye are justified in the name of the Lord Jesus, and by the Spirit of our God." Salvation calls us away from sinful lifestyles and empowers us by God's Spirit to refuse participation in sinful habits. It is only a part of the Christian's past, not his or her present way of life. That is why salvation is called "conversion." "Old things are passed away; behold, all things are become new" (2 Corinthians 5:17).

So, the excuse-maker will ask if it is possible to drink alcohol occasionally (not habitually) and still be saved. If you are asking that, I must shake my head. Why is it so hard to grasp God's definition here? Intoxicated means you are affected by an intoxicating substance. Christians do not do that anymore, do not want to do that anymore, realize the stern warnings from God about such behavior, and have put off the works of darkness in their lives. Of course Christians fall into sin (backsliding), are tempted to sin, are sometimes ensnared by the devil to sin, but sin is no longer a welcomed habit for the child of God. (See Romans 8:2) I was driving down the road the other day and noticed a sign over the freeway that said, "A buzz is still drunk driving." The world calls it a "buzz" but God calls it a sin.

Perhaps a logical element will help us grasp the point. If you drink a teaspoon of alcoholic beverage, you are a teaspoon drunk. If you drink one beer, you are one beer drunk. If you drink one small goblet of wine you are one small goblet intoxicated. Is God less strict in His standards than the officer of the law? Police administer a breathalyzer on the side of the road and issue DUI tickets for anything measuring .08 on the monitor. I have been told and have confirmed by research that two beers are enough to put you over the legal limit for blood alcohol. Is God less holy than the police officer? Is God confused and misled about the state of intoxication and we need to set Him straight? Ridiculous thoughts - and God will not be mocked!

Galatians 5:21 calls "drunkenness" a "work of the flesh." That same passage tells us that if Christians "walk in the Spirit" they will not "fulfill the lust of the flesh." Paul then gives a list of 17 things that are included in these "works of the flesh." Then the apostle strictly reminds the

Galatian believers that "they which do such things shall not inherit the kingdom of God."

Dear Christian, would you risk eternity for your beer? Would you really trade in your home in Heaven for your wine bottle? Too many professing saints cling to the false hope of "eternal security," thinking they can do what they want because God has to keep them saved. According to 2 Timothy 1:12, God can only "keep" that which has been "committed." If you do not have enough commitment and change in your life to heed James 1:27 which says pure religion is keeping oneself "unspotted from the world," you should not ever think you are eternally secure. At best, you are on a shaky foundation. At worst, you are blindly headed to Hell through the door of compromise and rebellion.

Drunkenness/intoxication is a soul-damning sin just like the perversion of homosexuality. Why would Christians willingly choose such a path? They wouldn't if they're truly a child of God. So, if someone calls himself a Christian, yet justifies drinking alcohol as a permissible indulgence of life, he needs to hear seriously the Matthew 7:23 warning for the religiously deceived, "And then will I profess unto them, I never knew you: depart from me, ye that work iniquity."

Some people hold their liquor pretty well. J. C. was that kind of man. His folks were just good ol' fashioned people who loved the Lord and ran a country store. They had not been in church for two weeks. I decided to stop by and check on them. As I stepped up to the trailer door, I was quickly made aware of their profligate son's revelry. I could hear from inside the trailer, "J. C. get off your mother; J. C. stop hurting your mother." I had already heard that this rebel of a son had to be shot with a shotgun by his dad to keep him from killing his mother while in a drunken stupor.

I knew I had to do something but this man was big. I felt I was no match for him. I prayed and remembered the story of Samson as I stormed in the door uninvited. The dad and mom were glad to see me. J. C. wasn't. He leaped across a twenty foot path in what seemed like a millisecond and was standing in my face with a 357 long barrel pistol pointed at my head. The drunkard said, "Preacher, I could kill you right now." I felt the boldness of the Holy Spirit well up within me and I spoke before I gave it a thought. "J. C., you can't do anything God won't permit you to do. Now put that gun down and go into that bedroom. I want to talk to you about Jesus." It was as though a million guardian angels slapped his arms down. He dropped that gun to his side, his arm limp. We went to the bedroom. He was still clinging to the gun. I told him, "Put that gun down now because I want to talk to you about Jesus." I was so glad to see that gun laid on the floor.

J. C. was a man who could drink a case of beer and talk to you as if he was stone-cold sober. The difference was in his breath, his body temperature, and his angered spirit. He was out to prove to the whole town that nobody could match his strength. He carried a sawed-off 45 caliber machine gun around with him in the seat of his truck. That's another story. But as I shared the plan of salvation with J. C. his heart melted. Yet, he was not ready to be saved. He said to me at the conclusion of my witness to him what countless others have said over the years: "I'm just not ready today." When is a man ready to be saved? The answer is when he realizes he is a sinner before God. God brings that awareness and God brings the grace that is needed to cover all our sins through Christ's blood which washes them all away. You simply cannot put God on your "waiting schedule." 2 Corinthians 6:2 says, "Behold, now is the accepted time; behold, now is the day of salvation."

Realizing J. C. would not come to Christ that afternoon, I obeyed a prompting from God's Holy Spirit. I asked the man if I could pray for him. He agreed. I prayed, "Dear Lord, this man is a great sinner, but not anymore than me or any other man in the world. I've told him how to get saved by trusting Jesus Christ for the forgiveness of sins, but he will not pray to be saved today. So, God, I want you to make this man the most miserable man in all the world. I'm asking you to not let him sleep or eat until he gives his heart to Christ and throws away his beer. In Jesus name I pray and Amen."

I left the home. That was a Friday. The very next Sunday, J. C.'s dad came to me in church and said, "You need to go see my son again. He hasn't been able to sleep or eat. He hasn't touched a bite of food. He hasn't slept a wink at night for two nights. Go see him again, please." I assured the dad that I would see his son real soon. I had to travel for an emergency surgery of another church member on that Monday, and I called to tell this family that I would come by when I got back from the hospital. When I got back the dad was rejoicing on the phone with me saying, "J. C. couldn't wait. He called another preacher and gave his heart to the Lord. He wants to be baptized in the river and wants you and the other preacher to do it."

It was a fine request because J. C. was so big it took two preachers to put him under the water. I felt like holding him down under a little longer for that stunt of putting a pistol to my head. I don't know whatever happened to J. C. I know he died. I know he has met his eternal destiny. I can only hope he threw his booze away for good, because the man that finds himself hooked to the bottle or the beer can has a lot of "contentions" according to Solomon plus a horrible place to go for the unchanged sinner.

Chapter Thirteen

Three Biblical Motives for Total Abstinence

What motivates people to drink alcohol? Virtually every source - medical, addiction recovery, psychological counselors, religious agencies, personal experience - state that drinking alcohol is an acquired taste. Psychologist Nathalie Serrels wrote:

> What you must realize is this: our bodies are actually very efficient at managing pain and suffering. When we drink a toxin, our brain and body becomes confused. In a manner of speaking, it begins to act as if we are not taking the toxin intentionally. Why? Because why ON EARTH would we consume a toxin willingly, especially if it didn't taste good? So our body then begins to make this "forced poisoning", so to speak, more pleasant. That's the acquired taste of alcohol.[36]

What science has discovered and the Bible affirms is that it moves from an acquired taste to a required taste. Addiction is measured by participation regardless of the baseless and counterproductive theories circulating in the secular recovery agencies. They cannot deny that if there had been no participation there could never have occurred an addiction. Man is constantly seeking to avoid guilt and accountability for his own sins and the consequences of those sins. So, the alcohol recovery

---

[36] Nathalie Serrels, "Alcohol is an Acquired Taste," Recovery Navigation. https://recoverynavigation.com/alcohol-is-an-acquired-taste-so-why-do-we-bother/#.W2HIV1uPLIU

centers provide at least two diversions in order to ignore the success of faith-based treatment. Greed motivates the secular, cognitive therapy centers because they need repeat clients.

First, they claim that varying addiction levels are affected by ethnic background. American Indians have the highest rate of alcoholism of any population group in America. 1 in 3 Native Americans who drink become alcoholics.[37] However, there are contributing factors besides ethnicity that explain this high rate. Poor education, fetal alcohol syndrome, low self esteem, and the rarely mentioned penchant for hallucinatory religious experience in animism, pantheism, and Shamanism all contribute to the motivation for this people group to use alcohol indiscriminately. Alcoholism is highest in their group because of participation.

Contrasted with Native Americans, only 1 in 15 Jews who drink alcohol will become alcoholics, now rephrased as "problem drinkers" to make it more socially acceptable.[38] The latest claim is that the Jew has the ADH1B gene which causes them to have unpleasant reactions to alcohol creating a deterrent. Despite the fact that only twenty percent of Jews have this gene, researchers like Deborah Hasin, Ph.D. of Columbia University, still claim genetics is more of a factor for low alcoholism rates among Jews than religion.[39]

Recovery advocates line up in a chain of liars who ignore the real truth to keep their multi-million dollar business in play. The real truth about low alcoholism among Jews is that great shame is associated with

---

[37] See https://pubs.niaaa.nih.gov/publications/arh22-4/253.pdf

[38] Statistic given to me at Cincinnati Alcoholic Hospital seminar in 1981. (See also Glassner B., Berg B. (1985) Jewish-Americans and Alcohol. In: Bennett L.A., Ames G.M. (eds) The American Experience with Alcohol. Springer, Boston, MA. https://doi.org/10.1007/978-1-978-1-4899-0530-7_7)

[39] Buddy Tee, "Rare Gene Discourages Alcoholism Among Jews," Very Well Mind. https://www.verywellmind.com/rare-gene-discourages-alcoholism-among-jews-63179.

drinking among their peoples. The practice for centuries of diluting their wines, rabbinic emphasis on moderation, and religious convictions all compose the picture for temperance among the chosen race. It is a simple fact that the Jews frown on drunkenness. The reports coming out of California and New York indicate a higher percentage of participation among this race yet the rate of clinical alcoholism is now below 1 percent.[40] Yet, the spurious science of the profligate Gentile race continues to perpetuate both the problem and the failing cure. The claim of genetic disposition or unreported, secret participation by those who refuse the obvious truth falls on deaf ears.

We are told that stress, peer pressure, fun, inhibitions, curiosity, accessibility, and preference are the reasons people choose to drink alcohol. Note that! Alcoholism is not a disease, a synaptic failure in the brain which, according to the rehabilitation experts, makes it impossible for the drinker to stop drinking. It is a choice to drink alcohol that Proverbs 23:32 says "in the end it bites like a snake." For some the end comes sooner than expected. For others, the venom never leaves because they have not found the fullness of the anti-venom at Calvary. For our purpose in this work we want to know if the Bible has any compelling motivation for the Christian to follow complete abstinence. It does! It does! It does! Three times we discover a call from God for the Christian to never touch wine or strong drink.

First, there is the call to preserve the Christian identity.

Romans 13:12-14 is clear: "The night is far spent, the day is at hand: let us therefore cast off the works of darkness, and let us put on the armour of light. Let us walk honestly, as in the day; not in rioting and drunkenness, not in chambering and wantonness, not in strife and envying. But put ye on the Lord Jesus Christ, and make not provision for the flesh, to fulfil the lusts thereof." For a Christian to consume alcohol brings into play three deliberate acts of disobedience to God. The inebriated Christian is wearing the works of darkness, walking dishonestly in drunkenness, and making provision for the flesh to

---

[40]Glassner, B. https://doi.org/10.1007/978-1-978-1-4899-0530-7_7

follow the lust of that fleshly desire. How is that possible? It is a denial of one's identity. Let us examine each one carefully.

Paul identifies the Christian as one who wears Jesus Christ. Some Christians, actually so called Christians, have a quick-change wardrobe wearing light and darkness interchangeably for whatever the occasion dictates. The Christian identity is not one of occasion but of established conviction. Inebriation, intoxication, drunkenness are all the same by Biblical definition and unfit to wear for the Christian. Next, a drinking Christian is a dishonest Christian. They claim to be a sober saint spiritually but drinking alcohol cancels their claim. They have an identity crisis. Finally, Christians who drink alcohol are giving in to the lusts of the flesh. The lusts of the flesh are many but this passage specifically names drinking alcohol alongside rioting. The critic who wishes to justify a pleasurable moment of inebriation accuses the glutton for doing the same thing. Whereas gluttony is a defiling sin, surely you can recognize the inequity of the comparison. When in the world has the consumption of three cheeseburgers caused a driver to veer recklessly into oncoming traffic and kill people? When did a person get his girlfriend drunk on extra tacos and pizza where he could rape her? Tacos, pizza, or cheeseburgers don't alter a person's consciousness. Alcohol does!

Christians need to remember that the flesh will be just as active as we allow it to be. Preserving the Christian identity was a chief concern of the apostle Peter when he wrote:

> Forasmuch then as Christ hath suffered for us in the flesh, arm yourselves likewise with the same mind: for he that hath suffered in the flesh hath ceased from sin; That he no longer should live the rest of his time in the flesh to the lusts of men, but to the will of God. For the time past of our life may suffice us to have wrought the will of the Gentiles, when we walked in lasciviousness, lusts, excess of wine, revellings, banquetings, and abominable idolatries: Wherein they think it strange that ye run not with them to the same excess of riot, speaking evil of you (1 Peter 4:1-5).

Do not think the phrase "excess of wine" permits moderate drinking. *Oinophlugia* in the Greek simply means "to bubble up and overflow." It is a play on words, common to Biblical writers, speaking of the bubbly nature of alcoholic wine. I refer you back to Chapter Twelve to define drunkenness. Yet, Peter said Christians do not walk this way, live this way, or act this way. On the contrary, they do not even run with people who do, causing those who drink to speak evil of the Christian living the separatist, holy life. Christians should be different inwardly and outwardly.

<u>Second, there is the call to protect the Christian influence</u>.

Romans 14:21 speaks in the context of offending or causing a Christian brother or sister to stumble by our actions. "It is good neither to eat flesh, nor to drink wine, nor any thing whereby thy brother stumbleth, or is offended, or is made weak." The apostle Paul addressed this concern also in 1 Corinthians 9. He said, "But take heed lest by any means this liberty of yours become a stumblingblock to them that are weak." Paul spoke of eating meat that had been offered to idols, to the Corinthian gods, and then sold in the marketplace. There is both a similarity and a difference between that and alcohol. Alcohol, in the average store in America, has not been offered to idols, unless you consider that the whole liquor industry itself is a salute to the ancient gods such as the Egyptian god of beer and wine (Osiris), and the Greek god of wine (Bacchus). However, drinking alcohol glorifies Satan rather than Jehovah God, making alcohol comparable to meat offered to idols.

What is the timeless principle of truth in Romans 14 and 1 Corinthians 9 for the Christian today? Namely this: if drinking alcohol causes another person, Christian or otherwise, to stumble, be offended, be put off from the Church, the claims of Christ, or the life-changing gospel of Christ, no person should drink alcohol and commit that offense against another human being. What do you think happens when a non-Christian sees a Christian in the restaurant sipping their mixed drink, or sees a Christian serving wine and beer at a wedding, or sees a Christian carrying a six-pack out of a store? Does this offend? Does this cause someone to stumble and be put off from being saved? Does this provide the unbeliever a point of contention with the message of the Bible? Does it provide the unbeliever an excuse to continue in sin? Yes, it can and often it does! Saints cannot be salt and light in this world and do those things.

Third, there is the call to prevent the cursed infirmity.

Thirty-five hundred years ago God sent a message to the Israelites in Exodus 15:26. "If thou wilt diligently hearken to the voice of the LORD thy God, and wilt do that which is right in his sight, and wilt give ear to his commandments, and keep all his statutes, I will put none of these diseases upon thee, which I have brought upon the Egyptians: for I am the LORD that healeth thee."

Any medical doctor, who will not lie, will tell you that the introduction of alcohol into the body system immediately shuts down the natural function of every vital organ because they have to stop and filter out the toxic poison of alcohol. Long term, we know that alcohol consumption causes cirrhosis of the liver, anemia, cardiovascular disease, dementia, seizures, gout, high blood pressure, suppression of the immune system, nerve damage, pancreatitis, gastritis, kidney disease, stroke, and other complicated infirmities. To knowingly disobey God's directive in Proverbs 23 and other passages previously cited is to invite a whirlwind of health problems. Do not swallow the lie that a little alcohol is profitable for your health. Whatever it aids is a tradeoff for double the amount of problems. Listen to God alone when He says in 1 Corinthians 3:17, "If any man defile the temple of God, him shall God destroy; for the temple of God is holy, which temple ye are." The physical body of a Christian is the temple of God's Spirit. There is a high price to pay in defiling with alcohol the vessel that is to be a pure and holy dwelling for God's Holy Spirit. Plenty have reaped this judgment for secretly or openly corrupting their body with the toxic poison of alcohol. No one can ever say that God didn't warn us.

Countless times I have witnessed people who claim they are Christians yet drink alcohol in public with no regard for their witness, their body, or the offense to God. I have looked across a restaurant and discovered a familiar face with their hand gripping the wine goblet. I have stumbled, I believe by Divine Providence, on a Christian trying to hide their beer from the preacher. Old time preachers would rebuke the drinker in public, even call the parents of a wayward child caught in a drunken party. I have to confess that my spirit is weakened at the sight of a Christian drinking. I am stunned by the hypocrisy. Regrettably, I have no boldness to reprove and rebuke. I should admonish and seek to restore the fallen saint but my faith is so offended at the sight that I am spiritually catatonic until I can discuss it with another like-minded Christian. At that point I have become a backbiter of the sipping, sinning saint. I do not like the effect.

Alcohol is a divider, an instigator of mischief and misery. God's people ought to shun it with all their might if for nothing else than to keep their testimony pure and their God unprovoked. You never know who may be watching. Some may have an in-your-face attitude to preserve their right to a beer or a glass of wine. If their church approves of it, the matter worsens, but what will you say when God takes it up with you for defiling your body, killing your witness, and disobeying His Word?

Chapter Fourteen

Timothy's Medicine Cabinet

I commonly hear advocates of wine and beer consumption justify their behavior by claiming, "Paul told Timothy to drink wine." So, along with the slippery slopes of claiming older women are permitted to drink alcohol and the blasphemous assertion that Jesus made, drank, and served alcohol, the apostle Paul is now roped into supporting the claims of the liberal, lying, hooch hawkers. To make these claims is to prove beyond a shadow of a doubt Bible ignorance.

Bible ignorance, more often than not, comes from a surface level knowledge that would barely fill a thimble without a microscopic speck of proper interpretation of the Scriptures. To use the old adage, "They know just enough to be dangerous." A cogent illustration will suffice.

If a person goes to another country which speaks a different language such as English to Spanish, he will have to acquire an interpreter. The interpreter knows the native language and can be the key to communication. Opening the Bible with the ability to read the English version is nowhere near the qualifications needed to ascertain proper meaning. Just as an interpreter is needed to properly translate Spanish to English, a study of the historical and cultural background of any Bible text is critical for understanding its meaning. Specifically, you need a linguistic tool to help examine the original intent of the author. However, a basic peek at 1 Timothy 5:23, "Drink no longer water, but use a little wine for thy stomach's sake and thine often infirmities," reveals some unmistakable facts on the surface. Common sense will discover the truth if the heart is open to receive the truth.

First of all, Paul's instruction to Timothy indicates there was something wrong with the water in first century Bible days, and therefore Paul was concerned about the water's effect on his beloved co-laborer. Second, Timothy had some stomach problems. Third, his stomach problems and other possible "infirmities" were very frequent problems for the evangelist/pastor. Fourth, and most important of all, the quantity of permissible wine to clear up the problem was "little," not much. Finally, the very fact that Paul stopped in the midst of discussing the conduct of elders, the concern for widows, and the crisis of open sin in the Church to counsel Timothy about wine for his stomach most certainly broadcasts that Timothy was an abstainer from alcohol. These general observations are a good starting point in understanding the true intent of the passage. One thing is for sure. This is not an open door to the tavern, nor a ticket to the alcoholic party for anybody.

It is likely that there was something wrong with the water in Bible days. Numerous sources confirm this fact as Jaeggli documented:

> During the Hellenistic through the Roman-Byzantine period, it is known that the Jews, like the ancient Greeks and Romans, avoided strong, concentrated wine, which the Talmud calls *yayin hai* (living wine); instead they drank only wine that had been mixed with water. This was not only to avoid becoming intoxicated, but also because diluted wine was healthier than plain water, which was known to be contaminated.[41]

Even today, if you travel to other countries, you may want to drink only bottled water to avoid pollutants and harmful organisms. The health hazzards are disastrous. I have personally experienced these hazards more than once while on mission work in Peru. However, such does not grant you permission to drink modern wines or beers in Germany, Italy, or other countries because their water "might" be contaminated. Bottled water is usually available in plentiful supply. The context here is that Timothy had an affliction. Unless you can testify of a stomach affliction there is no warrant from this Bible text to yield to the lust of a German beer full of Bavarian brew which sometimes boasts of a 16-17 percent

---

[41] Jaeggli, 15.

alcohol content just because you're in a country where the water is suspect. Bottled water is available, even in Germany.

There is no way to prove, other than assumption, that Timothy's "often infirmities" went beyond the stomach affliction. The fact that Paul mentions the stomach and "thine often infirmities" in the same sentence at least opens the possibility of other internal physical problems for Timothy. Yet, the point must be made, despite any lingering considerations of other unknown infirmities for the preacher, that Paul categorically did not tell Timothy, "Take a little wine for thy nerves' sake," or "Take a little wine for thy pleasure's sake," or "Take a little wine for thy heart's sake," or "Take a little wine for thy upper respiratory infection's sake." Let us adopt the strict Biblical stance. In this text abstinence is only rescinded for a stomach affliction due to impure water.

We accept the consideration of wine for medicine given a medical doctor made the prescription, yet the believer who uses it for medicine must be circumspect, Biblically sensitive to preserving a pure testimony and scientifically wise as to the risks. A recent study by researchers at the New York University School of Medicine found that one alcoholic drink per day has been proven to increase the risk of mouth, head, neck, and gastrointestinal cancers significantly.[42] Doctors are not the final authority in Christian conduct. The Word of God is that final authority, and we must not make Scripture say more than it does. Wine, the diluted kind of Bible days, is only authorized for severe stomach afflictions. 1 Timothy 5:23 must not be abused to justify drinking alcohol indiscriminately and capriciously for pleasure or pain.

Every word in the Bible is inspired according to 2 Timothy 3:16. For sure, the most inspired word in 1 Timothy 5:23, when it comes to the abstinence debate, is the word "little." Diluted three to four times with water, Timothy's wine would have been of very low alcoholic content, if any. The word used is *oinos*, a single word of choice in the New Testament, which can mean either fermented or unfermented wine

---

[42] AFP/Relaxnews, "One Drink A Day Can Increase Cancer Risk" https://www.newsmax.com/health/health-news/alcohol-drink-daily-cancer/2018/04/25/id/856518/.

depending on the context. Paul very well could have been saying to Timothy to take a little grape juice for his stomach's sake. However, such an abnormal mention of the matter in the text probably indicates a fermented wine diluted at least twenty-five percent with water.

Alcohol is a basic sterilizer, a killer of contaminates. As a medicine there may be some positive effects for its use inside the gastric chambers of the body that are inflamed and infested with harmful bacteria. Yet, there is no need to introduce alcohol into the system when a natural ingredient within grape juice will suffice to handle many stomach abnormalities. Peter Masters brought some enlightening insight to the value of wine in the stomach:

> It is now believed medically that wine releases acid in the stomach, which kills salmonella and other organisms, including *Helicobacter pylori*, which cause stomach ulcers. However, this wine must be strictly limited to avoid stomach inflammation. A component called resveratrol (found in grape skins) also benefits. It is interesting that several reputable medical surveys have shown that unfermented grape juice gives just the same benefit as wine.[43]

We need to consider one last point: the quantity of medicine recommended by Paul. How hard is it to understand the apostolic prescription, "use a little wine"? For specification, we must appeal to the linguistic principle. Of the three primary words for "little" in Greek, the first two - *braxus* and *mikros* - indicate a small measurement of time, distance, or stature. Zacchaeus, in Luke Nineteen, is referred to as "little of stature." *Mikros* is the word used to describe the short man who climbed the tree to see Jesus. Several words in the English language are associated with this *mikros,* such as microscope and microbes. It denotes something visually and impressively small. *Braxus* is the key word in Greek that refers to time, space or distance. But Paul's admonition to Timothy uses the Greek term *oligos* which has nothing to do with stature, time, or distance.

---

[43]Peter Masters, *Should Christians Drink: The Biblical Case for Abstinence* (London: Sword and Trowel, 1992), 23-24.

Oligos is the chief word which speaks of something notably small in amount by volume or quantity. It is the word that speaks of the "few fishes" that were used to feed the thousands on the mountain in Galilee (Matthew 15:34). Amongst the vast crowd the young lad's "puny" lunch hardly seemed sufficient. It is the word that speaks of the "few that find" the gate that leads to life (Matthew 7:14). It is a word of contrast and comparison to exemplify the "smallness" of the amount referenced. Therefore, it is with the authority of the word meaning in 1 Timothy 5:23 that we can forthrightly refute any explanation that justifies substantial consumption of alcohol as a medicine. Paul never counseled such. Timothy did not keep a whiskey bottle in his medicine cabinet to make cough medicine. Timothy did not cherish his wine bottle in the refrigerator. Timothy most certainly did not go sipping cocktails with the deacons at a local restaurant. He had to be urged, persuaded, even coaxed to break his regular abstinence routine to take a very small amount of diluted wine or grape juice to deal with chronic stomach ailments, nothing more. Once again, there is no approval from God in 1 Timothy 5:23 for drinking beverage alcohol freely and frivolously.

Chapter Fifteen

What Was Served In The Upper Room?

Given that we have established that Jesus never made alcoholic wine at Cana, it would be unreasonable to think He would break stride with His holy character in serving alcohol at the Last Supper. Yet, there are still those who insist that Jesus was a poison peddler, a maitre d' of the cabernet. Such is an insult to Christ's deity. Catholics, Lutherans, Episcopalians and some Christian churches serve alcoholic wine at their Communion Services. Their argument is that Jesus had to serve wine in the upper room because Passover was celebrated in the spring, grapes were harvested in the fall, and no grape juice would last that long in the unfermented state. Nothing could be further from the truth.

William Patton thoroughly documented the knowledge of the Jews on preventing fermentation in the grape juice. Jews preserved grape juice by boiling the juice to a thick syrup; sealing the juice in a vessel and submerging it in water, thereby depriving it from all oxygen: filtering out the gluten and yeast: or lowering the temperature to 45 degrees such as storing it in caves or in the depths of cold water lakes. These measures allowed the grape juice to remain sweet and unfermented for a whole year.[44]

The most provocative discovery about the upper room scene is not that Jesus was never forced to serve alcohol but is instead that He did not intend to serve alcohol. The language of the Bible proves that what Jesus served to His disciples, in that most holy moment where He described His

---

[44]Patton, *Bible Wines or the Laws of Fermentation and Wines of the Ancients*, 24-39.

upcoming death, was without doubt grape juice. The primary word for wine, *oinos*, in the New Testament is used 33 times. Yet, the distinguishing description of the drink at the Passover meal where the Lord's Supper was instituted never once mentions *oinos*. The absence of *oinos* is palpable and revealing. In the three synoptic Gospels, the Bible records the Passover and the Lord's Supper along with the Lord's instructions for our observance. Surely one of the Gospel evangelists would have used the prime word *oinos* for wine in their manuscript had there been fermented wine that night. It is strikingly missing.

Matthew 26:19 says His disciples "made ready the Passover." This feast had been celebrated by the Jews for over 1500 years. It is unthinkable that the disciples did not know to get alcoholic wine if that was the proper drink for the feast. It was not! In all three gospels, Matthew, Mark, and Luke, the simple word "cup" is mentioned and the distinguishing mark of the liquid on that table was referred to as "the fruit of the vine." Jesus said, as recorded by all three writers, "But I say unto you, I will not drink henceforth of this fruit of the vine, until that day when I drink it new with you in my Father's kingdom." If Christ had called it "wine" we would be forever in question as to whether alcohol was on that table or not. But He called it "the fruit of the vine." It is the nomenclature of distinction. The distinction notes the character of the drink. Nothing fits the phrase "fruit of the vine" accurately but grape juice.

Liberal sources claim that the phrase, "fruit of the vine" is a colloquialism which meant fermented wine to the Jew. Does this claim run true in other parts of the Bible where the words "fruit" and "vine" are used? For instance, the post-exilic prophet Zechariah brought hope to Israel as they were coming out of Babylonian captivity by telling them of God's plan to prosper them. "For the seed shall be prosperous; the vine shall give her fruit, and the ground shall give her increase, and the heavens shall give their dew; and I will cause the remnant of this people to possess all these things" (Zechariah 8:12). Is God saying here that the vine will produce an alcoholic drink? It doesn't fit. Other verses could be cited for reference but the conclusion would be redundant and perfectly clear. The "fruit of the vine" most assuredly was a colloquialism to speak of unfermented grape juice. This point was indisputably proven by the inspired words of Christ when He refused to call it *oinos* at the Last Supper table.

A simple linguistic examination of the words "fruit" and "vine" also pinpoints the non-alcoholic nature of the Passover juice. Fruit is *gennema* in Greek and speaks of that which is "generated." It is the initial product generated from the source origin. It is not a product of a product of a product. The fruit and the juice of that fruit were synonymous in the Jewish mind as Numbers 13:27 indicates. The spies who investigated Canaan came back and gave a report to Moses saying, "we came unto the land whither thou sentest us, and surely it floweth with milk and honey; and this is the fruit of it." It was the time of the first ripe grapes and they described it in liquid terminology. Milk and honey flow. So do grapes. They begin flowing the moment they are picked. The draining juice of the grape as it lay in the winepress was called "must" and was the most prized sweet juice to the Jewish palate. There is absolutely no license to consider *gennema* to include fermented juice because the dedicated root meaning is also used to speak of Jesus in John 3:16. Christ is the *monogenes*, only begotten, only generated Son of God. Just as Christ is the single one only of His kind generated of the same essence of the Father, so the unfermented juice of the grape is the only substance of its kind initially discharged from the grape. Vines do not produce fermented alcoholic beverages. They produce the pure sweet grape, which if corrupted and defiled, produces vinegar and alcohol.

In addition to the strict phrasing we can do a quick analysis of the elements of the Passover to know this was not alcoholic wine. The Passover elements used to institute the memorial were designed to picture the holy and sinless Lamb of God who came to take away the sins of the world. The bread was unleavened bread. Leaven was an emblem of evil, sin, and corrupting influence. Jesus said, "Beware of the leaven of the Pharisees and of the Sadducees" (Matthew 16:6) Paul warned of the legalistic doctrines of the Judaizers when he wrote in Galatians 5:9, "A little leaven leaveneth the whole lump." For fourteen days the Jewish homes searched their homes and made sure there was no leaven in the house when they celebrated the Feast of Unleavened Bread which preceded the Passover Feast (Exodus 12:15-19). If they were that strict how could anybody believe that alcoholic wine would be the companion to unleavened bread in the Passover?

Jesus said, "Take, eat, this is my body which is broken for you; this do in remembrance of me." The only lamb permissible for the Passover meal was an unblemished lamb (Exodus 12:5). Jesus had no sin. Likewise, the cup symbolized His blood. His blood was pure. All men from Adam have tainted blood. The fermented wine, soured with microbes of putrefaction and decay, would have been a mocking symbol of Christ's fitness as the Substitutionary Sacrifice for our sins. Righteous blood atoned for the unrighteous. There was no alcohol involved at this table and there will not be any when He drinks it new in His Father's Kingdom. So, if you're planning to get alcoholic wine, head-buzzing beer, or liver-killing liquor in the afterlife, you'll have to go somewhere besides heaven.

Chapter Sixteen

Troublesome Passages

If we take the position that God demands total abstinence from us, we have to address the following passages and deal with any seeming difficulties:

Genesis 14:18	2 Samuel 16:2
Genesis 27:28	Job 1:13
Genesis 27:37	Job 32:19
Genesis 49:11-12	Psalm 104:15
Exodus 29:40	Ecclesiastes 9:7
Leviticus 23:13	Song of Solomon 5:1
Numbers 6:20	Song of Solomon 7:9
Deuteronomy 14:26	Isaiah 55:1
Deuteronomy 28:39	Jeremiah 13:12
Deuteronomy 32:38	Jeremiah 31:12
Judges 19:19	Zechariah 9:17
1 Samuel 1:24	Acts 2:13
1 Samuel 25:18	Revelation 14:10

These 26 verses are troublesome. At first glance, you might read them and doubt that God is against alcohol. However, once adequately explained, these verses are consistent with God's call to abstinence. Yet, even as you compare the 26 difficult verses to the 286 verses on wine and strong drink, both in the Old and New Testaments, you have less than ten percent of the passages that might raise questions as to God's stance on alcohol. Let's examine the verses in question to banish all doubt.

Genesis 14:18: "And Melchizedek king of Salem brought forth bread and wine: and he was the priest of the most high God."

Melchizedek is a mysterious character in the Word of God. He is mentioned here in Genesis. Then he is mentioned in Psalm 110. There is another passage in Hebrews 5 which unravels the mystery of his character to a greater degree but not completely. All in all, Melchizedek is mentioned 11 times in the Bible. Who is he? Without examining each detail, many scholars believe he is Jesus Christ, the great High Priest of our profession, which seems to be accurately proclaimed in Hebrews 5. This is also confirmed in John 8 where Jesus said, "Abraham rejoiced to see my day: and he saw it, and was glad." The Pharisees were shocked and angry that Jesus said that and replied, "Thou art not yet fifty years old, and hast thou seen Abraham?" Indeed He probably did see Abraham in the valley of Siddim when He came as Melchizedek, priest of the most High God, and received tithes from Abraham of all the spoils of battle he gained by defeating the four kings. Those appearances of Jesus in the Old Testament are called "Christophanies" or "Pre-Incarnate Appearances."

Abraham's great great grandson was Levi, of whose tribe were the priests of the Temple under the Levite Aaron. In essence, the Levites were paying tithes by proxy through his great great grandfather even before Levi was born. But Melchizedek, according to Hebrews 5, had neither "beginning of days, nor end of life; but made like unto the Son of God; abideth a priest continually." The Melchizedek priesthood supersedes the Levitical priesthood for many reasons, not the least of which is that the Melchizedek priesthood is eternal according to Hebrews 7:3. For these reasons, and many more, this Melchizedek is a complete mystery without any identification unless he is Jesus.

There are many pre-incarnate appearances of Jesus in the Old Testament. He had already appeared to Abraham twice before in Genesis 12:7 and Genesis 17:1. He appeared to Jacob at Peniel (Genesis 32:24-30). He appeared to Joshua at Jericho (Joshua 5:13; 6:2). There he is called a "man" with a sword drawn in his hand, and also "the Lord". There are numerous references to the "Angel of the Lord" in the Old Testament. Walter C. Kaiser, President Emeritus of Gordon Conwell Theological Seminary, wrote:

> These real occurrences, initiated by God, were characterized by the fact that they were convincing revelations of his person and work, as much as they were also transitory, fleeting, but audible and clearly visible appearances. He came temporally in the form of a human, much before his final incarnation as a babe in Bethlehem, yet this same "Angel of the LORD" is called and is addressed often as "the LORD/Yahweh" himself (Gen 12:7; 17:1; 19:1; etc.).This "Angel of the LORD" was a title that stood for his office, but it did not describe his nature. The Hebrew word for "angel" (mal'ak) had the basic idea of one who was "sent," a "messenger." Of the 214 usages of the Hebrew term used for "angel," about one-third of them refer to what is labeled by theologians as a "Christophany," a temporary appearance of Christ in the Old Testament.[45]

On this evidence, I believe Melchizedek is the one and only priest of His kind, Jesus Christ appearing first to Abraham. How interesting, then, is the recognition of the two elements of which Melchizedek blessed Abraham to partake: bread and wine, the same elements given for communion in the Lord's Supper. The word in this text is *yayin*, the prime word in the Old Testament for wine that has the possibility to intoxicate. Yet, we know and have proven that Jesus did not serve alcoholic wine for Communion in the New Testament. Why would He serve alcoholic wine to Abraham in the Old Testament? He would not! This is one of the few cases where *yayin*, according to context, has to be unfermented wine because the view that it is fermented alcoholic wine does not fit the full message of the Bible. (See explanation on Genesis 49:11)

Genesis 27:28: "Therefore God give thee of the dew of heaven, and the fatness of the earth, and plenty of corn and wine."

Here, God gives three things to man: the dew of heaven (nothing wrong with that), the fatness of the earth (nothing wrong with God-

---

[45] Walter C. Kaiser, "Jesus In the Old Testament," Gordon Conwell Theological Seminary Online. (See http://www.gordon conwell.edu/resources/Jesus-in-the-Old-Testament.cfm)

given fertility of the ground yielding a bountiful harvest), and plenty of corn and wine. The corn is certainly not fermented. Neither is the wine because the word here is *tiyrowsh*, not *yayin*. *Tiyrowsh*, almost without exception is unfermented wine in the Bible. God gives us things that are good for us. It does not say God gives us alcoholic wine.

Genesis 27:37: "And Isaac answered and said unto Esau, Behold, I have made him thy lord, and all his brethren have I given to him for servants; and with corn and wine have I sustained him: and what shall I do now unto thee, my son?"

Again, we find the word *tiyrowsh* here which means Jacob's blessing, stolen from Esau, included plenty of vineyards producing unfermented wine in the grape. Isaac had been deceived and blessed Jacob instead of Esau with a promised blessing on the crops of his land: corn and grapes.

Genesis 49:11-12: "Binding his foal unto the vine, and his ass's colt unto the choice vine; he washed his garments in wine, and his clothes in the blood of grapes: His eyes shall be red with wine, and his teeth white with milk."

This is Judah's blessing from the patriarch Jacob on his death bed. Jesus Christ was of the tribe of Judah, thus fulfilling the prophecy of the Messianic line that a "sceptre shall not depart from Judah, nor a lawgiver from between his feet, until Shiloh come" (Genesis 49:10). Shiloh is a cryptic reference to the coming Messiah because the word simply means "Peaceable One" to whom all the people will bow and obey. That is Jesus! This tribe will be so blessed that their vineyards will be so large and strong that a man can tie his animal to the vine and it will hold him. Now that is a pretty large vine. Jesus Christ called Himself "The Vine" in John 15:1. If you tie your life to Christ, He will be strong enough to hold you and satisfy you.

This verse is an example of Hebrew poetry which characteristically uses parallelism for structure. That is, the poet, instead of rhyming as in our English poetry, states two sentences that are talking about the exact same thing but using different descriptive words. "He washed his garments in wine, and his clothes in the blood of grapes" speaks of the same thing. So, whatever the wine is, it has to agree with the "blood of grapes." Blood is a metaphor for the color red coming from the grapes. That redness comes from the skin of the grape mixing with the juice. Even though the word *yayin* appears in this text, it is without question a usage that references an unfermented juice. The point of the passage is that Judah's vineyards will produce such an abundance of grapes that the people could wash their clothes in the grape juice and still have enough for everyone to drink it.

Exodus 29:40: "And with the one lamb a tenth deal of flour mingled with the fourth part of an hin of beaten oil; and the fourth part of an hin of wine for a drink offering."

The "drink offering" was to be offered with the "sweet savour offerings" according to Numbers 15. The drink offering was not to be observed until Israel had come into the Promised Land and all of their enemies had been defeated by the hand of God. This coincides with the fact that Jesus refused drink on the cross because it was mixed with gall (alcohol) and that He told his disciples he would not drink of the fruit of the vine until He drank it new in the kingdom. The earthly purpose of the drink offering was to symbolize our life of sin poured out upon Jesus on the cross. Remember that yeast was the unholy substance that represented man's sin. God's wrath was symbolized in the *yayin* (alcoholic wine) poured out on the unblemished sacrifice placed on the altar. In the same manner, as Jesus was being offered on the cross as a sacrifice for sin, the sinless Jesus took on Himself the unholy sins of man (2 Corinthians 5:21).

Note that the "drink offering" was never drunk by man, not even the priests. We might add that this is the best thing to do with alcohol today. Pour it out! The heavenly purpose of the drink offering was to give a prophetic portrait of Christ many years before His death on the cross. Isaiah 53:12 says that Christ "poured out his soul unto death." Yes, this drink offering was *yayin*, but it was not consumed by man's mouth. In the drink offering God rejoices in the completed work of Christ for our redemption. It also portrays God rejoicing in the blessed fruit of Christ's incarnation, His life, His death, His resurrection, His ascension and His glorification at God's right hand. Since the drink offering had to be poured out daily, a fermented wine was likely used.

But it was in the hands of the priest for the proper purpose. They would not dare drink it because to do so would mean immediate death (See Numbers 28:7). There is some thought that the alcohol may have killed bacteria and germs in this environment of blood.[46]

Leviticus 23:13: "And the meat offering thereof shall be two tenth deals of fine flour mingled with oil, an offering made by fire unto the LORD for a sweet savour: and the drink offering thereof shall be of wine, the fourth part of an hin."

The drink offering was always poured on the sacrificial animal at the brazen altar of sacrifice (see Genesis 35:14 and Philippians 2:17) and around that brazen altar but never at the altar of incense. There is a great reason for the stipulation given in Exodus 30:9 not to pour out a drink offering on the altar of incense. At the brazen altar, God celebrates with joy, not inebriated joy - hence unfermented *yayin*. Both altars are worship altars. However, the Brazen Altar is the altar that represents Christ's atoning work dying for the sins of humanity. The Altar of Incense represents the completed work of Christ arising to God as a sweet smelling incense, an aroma of perfect redemption through the blood. Christ's work at Calvary was a completed work, a pure work making grace available for all men who believe. That is separate from Christ's work now in heaven, symbolized at the altar of incense, the great intercession for us before the Father. Man cannot add anything to that. That work is beyond our belief and repentance, and totally inside the heart of Christ to save us to the uttermost (see Hebrews 7:25). Note that the meat offering (meal offering) was made by fire. It is comforting to know that there is a fire in Jesus' heart when He prays for us in heaven. Prayer needs no cleansing when offered by the Lord. Sacrifice for sin required a "pouring out" of Christ's blood. There is no shedding of blood in heaven. It was finished at Calvary.

---

[46] See http://www.hiscandleministry.com/2013/06/04/chapter-seven-drink-offerings-were-poured-out-as-a-burnt-sacrifice-never-consumed/

Numbers 6:20: "And the priest shall wave them for a wave offering before the LORD: this is holy for the priest, with the wave breast and heave shoulder: and after that the Nazarite may drink wine."

Chapter Four presented a Nazirite as a person who took a vow to be dedicated to the Lord. They could not drink any wine, alcoholic or otherwise. Not even grapes or raisins were permitted for consumption. Why? Their dedication to God required separation from anything that was considered by God to be evil or associated with evil and impurity.

In Amos 2 we find God angry with Israel, claiming they had transgressed (sinned) against him by giving their Nazirites *yayin* wine to drink. There were four Nazirites in the Bible: Samuel, Samson, Manoah's wife (which was Samson's mother), and John the Baptist. The Nazarite vow could either be temporary or permanent. John the Baptist was a permanent Nazirite and Jesus said that he was the greatest man ever born (see Matthew 11:11). Pay attention to that! A permanent vow of abstention from alcohol finds great favor with God.

Notice that this verse says the Nazirite "may drink wine" but he doesn't have to. A man may stick leaves in his mouth and set them on fire, filling his lungs and whole body with smoke, but it is most certainly foolish by all estimates of the outcome. If God wanted us to smoke tobacco, He surely would have made our nose out of bricks. If God wanted us to drink alcohol, He surely would have given us a copper stomach and liver.

Deuteronomy 14:26: "And thou shalt bestow that money for whatsoever thy soul lusteth after: for oxen, or for sheep, or for wine, or for strong drink, or for whatsoever thy soul desireth: and thou shalt eat there before the LORD thy God, and thou shalt rejoice, thou, and thine household."

The very sight of this verse reminds me of my grandfather, an alcoholic, functioning alcoholic at that, but a man who died bleeding internally from his alcoholism. I will never forget him quoting this verse to me and my dad as a justification for drinking alcohol. For some time, I wrestled with the meaning of this verse. Surely God was not approving an alcoholic lifestyle. Surely God was not condoning purchasing alcoholic wine in connection with the holy festivals of Israel. This verse is a classic case of misusing Scripture when the reader focuses more on the superficial meaning of a verse than on the context and true intention of the verse.

The intent of the passage is set in the anticipation of Passover. The prescription is all about giving tithes at the festival "in the place which he shall choose to place his name there" (See verse 23). That is a reference to Jerusalem. The Jewish tithes were not at all like our tithes. Theirs was an agricultural society where they tithed animals and crops. They gave unblemished animals and the firstfruits of their crops. We do not do that today. We do not bring spotless heifers, bulls, goats, birds, corn, and wine to our churches. So the passage, in essence, does not apply to us for two reasons. Christians do not celebrate Passover, and we do not tithe in the same manner as the Jews. We are not linked to the sacrificial system of Leviticus.

Secondly, note that this verse says "eat there," but it never says "drink there." The reason for that, as aforementioned, was that the drink offering of wine was poured out on the ground and on the burnt offering. Even if it was alcoholic it was not to be drunk. Furthermore, as we discussed earlier, the alcohol was to represent our corruption and sin that had to be poured out on Jesus as He took the penalty for our wickedness.

Thirdly, this passage indicates what is commonly called the "delayed tithe." The Passover was held in Jerusalem, the place where God put his name. There was a rival temple in Dan to the north of Jerusalem which was established by Jeroboam who worried that worshipers going south to celebrate the festival would lose their loyalty to him (1 Kings 12:26-29). God did not put his approval on the temple in Dan. Consequently, if a Jew wanted to please God, he had to travel to Jerusalem. The journey was time-consuming, expensive, and difficult for worshipers to travel with their animals and their crops to Jerusalem. (See verse 24 where it mentions "if the way be too long for thee.") The provision here is to sell their tithes for money, hold the money until they could get to Jerusalem, and then buy the necessary items for worship there in the holy city, one of which was alcohol for the priests to pour over the offering. It is not an approval of drinking alcoholic wine at all. It is a call to "fear the Lord thy God always" in worship, something a person cannot do when they are a winebibber and given to drinking alcohol. Remember, no person was permitted to drink alcohol when they came into the temple for worship (Leviticus 10:9).

Deuteronomy 28:39: "Thou shalt plant vineyards, and dress them, but shalt neither drink of the wine, nor gather the grapes; for the worms shall eat them."

Take no consolation in this verse to think God approves of alcoholic *yayin* wine. Deuteronomy 28 gives a full list of curses that God brings upon disobedient Israel. *Yayin* is grouped with "gathering the grapes" in this text. This may well be a sign of God's disapproval of fermented grape juice because the commandment of the Lord has been ignored. Israel was to be a holy nation and a peculiar people, and their lifestyle of idolatry and debauchery caused them to be made a "byword" among the nations (Deuteronomy 28:37). This verse is a judgment stating that worms would devour the vineyard fruit before it could ripen, much less ferment. This judgment is against alcohol. The Israelites were turning grape juice into alcohol, so God destroyed the vineyards. Often God ruins our plans and our projects when they are deliberately defying the Divine directive.

Deuteronomy 32:38: "Which did eat the fat of their sacrifices, and drank the wine of their drink offerings? let them rise up and help you, and be your protection."

This is obviously no warrant for drinking *yayin*, fermented wine. It is an expression of God's contempt and mockery of their idolatry. The substances used were the "fat of their sacrifices" and the wine of the drink offering. As aforementioned, the drink offering was to be poured out, not imbibed. Yet, these rebellious Israelites, in the belief that the idols of other gods ate and drank their offerings, participated in worship to the false deities by drinking the wine and eating the fat that should have been consumed by fire when offered to Jehovah. In verse 32, God calls the source of this wine offering the "vine of Sodom" and the "grapes of gall." That is God's view of the fermented drink, especially (but not exclusively) when it is offered to false deities.

Judges 19:19: "Yet there is both straw and provender for our asses; and there is bread and wine also for me, and for thy handmaid, and for the young man which is with thy servants: there is no want of any thing."

This verse is the welcome that a citizen of Gibeah gave to a Levite and his concubine who came to stay for the night. There was a lot wrong in Gibeah. Perverts, just like those in Sodom, abused this man's concubine all night. Then the strangest, most hideous action took place. The Levite took his defiled concubine, cut her up in twelve pieces, and sent those pieces to the twelve tribes of Israel to inflame them for vengeance. The only good thing in the story is an Ephraimite's hospitality when no one else would be hospitable to the traveling Levite. The Ephraimite offers *yayin* wine to his guests. Be for sure that the actions of men are not always the intentions of God. Do not make this passage out to be a positive affirmation of alcohol, even for hospitality sake. There is something of corruption in the whole story.

Verse 22 says that "as they were making their hearts merry" the perverts came knocking on the door. It very well could be they were making their heart merry with intoxicating beverage and their inebriated condition allowed the atrocities of perverted lust to transpire right under their noses. Moral restraint is relaxed under alcohol's influence. Alertness is dowsed and inoperative under the influence of alcohol. It would not be the first time or the last time somebody suffered greatly because their protectors were drunk.

1 Samuel 1:24: "And when she had weaned him, she took him up with her, with three bullocks, and one ephah of flour, and a bottle of wine, and brought him unto the house of the LORD in Shiloh: and the child was young."

Elkanah's family, which includes Hannah and Peninah, were devout people. They were country dwellers, and thus may have been prevented the annual visit to the temple in Jerusalem to offer sacrifices to God. Desiring to set the example with his family and offspring, Elkanah went to the place of worship and made the proper sacrifices. In this case, the offering was a peace offering, as indicated by the dividing of the portions and giving Hannah, one of his wives, the choice portion as an indication of her husband's favor. Peninah, the other wife, was of course peevish and provoking, an instigator of mayhem and thief of peace. Elkanah loathed this disharmony in his family and accordingly made the peace offering. Hannah followed in her husband's steps by devoting herself to God, worshiping by sacrifice, and fulfilling the vow she made to the Lord when she asked for a child.

Later, Hannah took Samuel, the child she had prayed for, when he was forty days old to the Tabernacle and dedicated him in service to the Lord. When the yong boy is weaned, a mere three years old, she brought the proper sacrifice for the time of release of her son. This dedicated child was to be raised among Eli's sons for Temple service. She brought three bullocks, one for a burnt offering, one for a sin offering and one for a peace offering. She was not sacrificing to make God indebted to her favor. She was sacrificing to appeal to God to receive her "living sacrifice," (see Romans 12:1-2) her son, as gratitude for God's gift of a son to her.

Along with the animals, Hannah brought the flour and wine that were the standard offering as prescribed by Moses in Leviticus 23. The wine was for a drink offering which accompanied the burnt offering. Once again, the *yayin* (fermented wine if it was not diluted) was poured out upon the meat of the burnt offering and around the altar. It was not consumed by humans. All of this was for consecration of the young Samuel to the Lord. Consecration and drunkenness do not mix.

1 Samuel 25:18: "Then Abigail made haste, and took two hundred loaves, and two bottles of wine, and five sheep ready dressed, and five measures of parched corn, and an hundred clusters of raisins, and two hundred cakes of figs, and laid them on asses."

Nowhere in this text does it say that the gift of two bottles of wine from Abigail's house was consumed by David or his soldiers for pleasure. Given the context, the *yayin* (fermented wine if not diluted) would have been used for medicine. I do not maintain that fermented wine did not exist in Bible days. Instead, we are identifying God's position on the usage. We know that Nabal, Abigail's husband, believed in drinking alcohol. He was a fool because his name actually means fool and his behavior proved he lived up to his name. The passage also says he was considered a "son of Beliel," a contemptuous term which means "worthless." Listen, you drinkers. Do you want to be known as, "worthless and a fool"? Nabal threw a fit if he didn't get his way. His servants despised him. His wife put up with him till God killed him. Abigail may have known no other life but the storing of fermented drink on her pantry shelf for her wicked husband. There is no smile from God in this passage on drinking fermented wine.

2 Samuel 16:2: "And the king said unto Ziba, What meanest thou by these? And Ziba said, The asses be for the king's household to ride on; and the bread and summer fruit for the young men to eat; and the wine, that such as be faint in the wilderness may drink."

Here, *yayin* is used as medicine to strengthen faint soldiers who traveled long times and distances in the wilderness desert. It may well have been Ziba's gift to David to use according to Proverbs 31:6. If a soldier was dying, wine was given to relieve the horror of death. Note that only one bottle of wine was given to David by Ziba, hardly enough for hundreds of soldiers to "drink and be merry." Perish the thought that God favors indiscriminate usage of the fermented, alcoholic drink. This passage doesn't support it.

Job 1:13: "And there was a day when his sons and his daughters were eating and drinking wine in their eldest brother's house."

This was what Job feared. Job, a "perfect and upright man, one that feareth God, and escheweth evil," according to God, was praying every morning for his children. Job "rose up early in the morning, and offered burnt offerings" every day. Why was Job doing this? The answer is stated in verse 5 of that text: "It may be that my sons have sinned, and cursed God in their hearts." Sure enough, Job was right! His sons and daughters had turned their backs on God and turned to the bottle. They were party animals. You can't be a party animal and love God at the same time. This verse gives a strict and sober warning about the alcohol life: God is angered by it. Judgment from the Lord can cut such a life short, and no amount of praying from a righteous parent can spare the profligate child from catastrophic and sovereign punishment due to drinking. Since God has warned of alcohol it is foolish to think He favors it in moderation. Job's family can testify of that from the grave. Many fathers have grieved deeply over their children who have sold their souls to the devil in drinking alcohol.

Job 32:19: "Behold, my belly is as wine which hath no vent; it is ready to burst like new bottles."

No approval of wine here. This is a description from Elihu about how his belly felt. Reading the context, you really understand that this passage is not about wine at all. Elihu was frustrated by the misguided arguments of Eliphaz, Bildad, and Zophar, and their failure to set Job straight. Elihu thought he had the answer and he has had a "belly full" of the others' reasoning. The image is fitting. Wine, when it is fermenting, sets off gasses as the yeast converts the sugar content to ethanol. This emission would swell a Biblical wine bottle which is made from the leg skin of a sheep. The skin was sewn up to seal it for storing liquid. Fermenting wine would swell the skin till it burst. Jesus used the same illustration to present His truth that His new teachings did not fit in the unchanged lives of the legalistic Pharisees. That is why He said that you don't put new wine into old wineskins. How ironic that the alcohol guzzlers call the teetotalers legalistic. That is an unfitting image. It gives the changed life of a Christian a "belly full" of the ignorance of those who champion drinking alcohol. No permission to drink booze in this text. Elihu is describing a physical condition that mimics what wine does to the wineskin.

Psalm 104:14-15: "He causeth the grass to grow for the cattle, and herb for the service of man: that he may bring forth food out of the earth; And wine that maketh glad the heart of man, and oil to make his face to shine, and bread which strengtheneth man's heart."

This is one passage in the Old Testament that shows *yayin* doesn't always mean fermented wine. We simply cannot divorce the word from the context. The context of "grass for cattle, herb for man, food out of the earth," clearly indicates the primordial product first issuing from agriculture. Since wine is included, the accurate interpretation of this *yayin* is juice from the grape. It may be entering fermentation, which explains the reason why the word *yayin* is used. How important it is to find the central message of these verses. We must be humble and thankful to God for all His provisions. One of those provisions is the fruit of the vine, in this case grapes. But it is the height of man's hubris to declare the alcoholic conversion of God's grapes is a blessing like unto the cattle and the food out of the earth. God condemns alcohol in Proverbs 20:1 and Proverbs 23:29-32, which cannot be connected with the wine here "that maketh glad the heart of man."

Ecclesiastes 9:7: "Go thy way, eat thy bread with joy, and drink thy wine with a merry heart; for God now accepteth thy works."

It is ironic that the word *yayin* appears in this text, for Solomon is giving the reason why people drink alcohol. They do not think that there is an afterlife where they will give an account to God. Instead, the wise king counsels, since you believe that life is meaningless, simply vanity and vexation of spirit, then live it up with eating, drinking and being merry. Drink the intoxicating wine, because if you believe that philosophy of life, then you are of the mistaken impression that this earthly sojourn is all you get. ? Have you become wise yet to the King's intent? It is a facetious counsel for the misguided to turn them around.

In the 1960s there was a commercial for Schlitz Beer which said, "You only go around once in life, so you've got to grab for all the gusto you can." It is a deceiving call to a hedonistic lifestyle based upon the false notion that there is nothing beyond the grave. A man had better hope that God "accepteth thy works" and justifies the wine-drinking, beer-guzzling, liquor-loving lifestyle because if there is a life beyond the grave where we will stand before a holy God and be judged for the deeds done in the body as the Bible says, the drinker who justifies what God doesn't is in deep, deep trouble.

Song of Solomon 5:1: "I am come into my garden, my sister, my spouse: I have gathered my myrrh with my spice; I have eaten my honeycomb with my honey; I have drunk my wine with my milk: eat, O friends; drink, yea, drink abundantly, O beloved."

This is a curious verse here in which Solomon referenced an ancient mixture of wine and milk. Yes, it is *yayin*, the intoxicating liquor of adults, but it is mixed with milk, the sobering liquid of infants. We have no way of knowing the percentage of dilution but if the practice mimics the dilution of wine with water, it could have been up to twenty times diluted with milk. Such a concoction would not inebriate and would not be taken with the intent for inebriation. Despite this explanation, every student of the Song of Solomon understands that the verses symbolize Solomon and his maiden and points to the greater companions, Christ and His bride. Solomon is speaking metaphorically of Christ's amazing joy with his bride compared to a drink of health and happiness. He is so overjoyed with the Bride that He invites us to share in his joy. How can an inebriated saint, who has defied His Word by getting literally intoxicated, demonstrate any joy with the Lord except it be in rank hypocrisy?

Song of Solomon 7:9: "And the roof of thy mouth like the best wine for my beloved, that goeth down sweetly, causing the lips of those that are asleep to speak."

The passage explains itself. The "best wine" for Solomon "goeth down sweetly." It is not sour. It does not burn. It is not dry because it goes down with ease in the sweetness. Dare not to defile the fullest meaning of the verse by saying the latter part speaks of the mumblings of someone in the sleep of a drunken stupor. This is not at all the king's intent. It is a clear commentary on the "best wine" of John 2. Alcohol makers know that the sugar is consumed by the yeast and converted to ethanol. Solomon's wine here is full of sugar, which means it is the fresh juice of the grape, another usage of *yayin* which is not fermented.

Isaiah 55:1: "Ho, every one that thirsteth, come ye to the waters, and he that hath no money; come ye, buy, and eat; yea, come, buy wine and milk without money and without price."

It is absolutely mind-boggling that anyone would take this passage which speaks about the freeness and fullness of God's offer of salvation and make it a verse of contention about drinking intoxicating wine because the word appears in the invitation. Yet, some overlook the message by focusing on a buzz in a bottle. In Bible days, intoxicating *yayin* was available for purchase. But the point of this passage is the contrast of the things in the world that do not satisfy with eternal things that do. People keep paying their money, their hard-earned money, for items of necessity and pleasure that bring only temporary enjoyment. Place that beside the grace of God that is life-releasing, the mercy of God that is undeserved, and the forgiveness of God that is free and liberating, and it becomes incredible that men only concern themselves with water, wine, milk and bread.

Three types of liquid are presented. First, waters. Note that it is plural. The full and abundant waters of salvation that never dry up are the waters that Jesus offered the woman at the well in John 4. This is the water that will cause a man to never thirst again. Second, wine. Yes, *yayin*, diluted or full strength, fermented or unfermented, sweet or sour. Buy all you want, drink all you want and you'll never know the joy that is in another vessel which surpasses all experiences from earth's bounty. There is nothing like the fullness of God's Holy Spirit.

I would encourage everyone to trade in the inebriating bottle that costs far more than the price tag on the deceptive label, and pay nothing for a drink in the Lord. Third, milk. This is the liquid of growth and development which every baby in the crib or in momma's arms squirms with impatient cries till the bottle is turned up on precious lips. Would to God that men would reject the anesthetic of alcohol and "desire the sincere milk" of God's Word. The latter costs nothing and satisfies everything. The booze is so costly that a man will never stop paying the grim wages of its destruction and defilement till every bottle and wine glass is tossed into the pit of hell from where it comes.

Jeremiah 13:12: "Therefore thou shalt speak unto them this word; Thus saith the LORD God of Israel, Every bottle shall be filled with wine: and they shall say unto thee, Do we not certainly know that every bottle shall be filled with wine?"

There is no glowing and glamorous image of wine in this text despite it being posted on the billboards and advertisements. A colorfully labeled bottle chucked into a bucket of ice cubes begging for the thirsty tongue to pop the cork is not in the least the message of Jeremiah to brazen and backslidden Israel. The prophet speaks of a nation God loves and would wear them close to his heart as a person wears an undergarment. Yet,"this evil people, which refuse to hear my words, which walk in the imagination of their heart, and walk after other gods, to serve them, and to worship them, shall even be as this girdle, which is good for nothing," is God's indictment (Jeremiah 13:10). This description is too close for comfort to those who refuse to hear what God says about alcohol in His word and instead "walk in the imagination of their heart." For those who do that, they can expect the same treatment which came to wayward Israel. They can expect that "every bottle will be filled with wine." This is one of several places in God's word where *yayin* wine is used as a symbol of staggering judgment from God.

If you recall the discussion in Chapter Ten, God uses wine as a symbol of judgment but also a symbol of joy. However, fermented wine is not favored by God. As the passage continues, God says He will fill the people with drunkenness so He can destroy them. God uses their love of alcohol to make them "dash one against another" until they are utterly destroyed (verses 13-14). Before God allows you to take the same path of a drunkard, as punishment for your sin of loving alcohol, trade that alcohol for the sweet, sober walk in righteousness with God. Rejecting beer, wine, and liquor for the "good gifts" from God is a wise choice (See James 1:17).

Jeremiah 31:12: "Therefore they shall come and sing in the height of Zion, and shall flow together to the goodness of the LORD, for wheat, and for wine, and for oil, and for the young of the flock and of the herd: and their soul shall be as a watered garden; and they shall not sorrow any more at all."

This is a message to the captives in Babylon that there is coming a day when they will be back in their land and "sing in the height of Zion." This is a complete turn around from Psalm 137:2 where they "hung their harps upon the willows." The question is whether the "goodness of the Lord" includes fermented wine. Forbid the thought because the wine in this text is *tiyrowsh*, unfermented sweet grape juice. If it had been fermented wine Jeremiah would have used the word *yayin*.

Zechariah 9:17: "For how great is his goodness, and how great is his beauty! corn shall make the young men cheerful, and new wine the maids."

Zechariah, as one of post-exilic prophets (after Israel came out of

Babylonian captivity), prophesied during the 6th century B.C. His message was one of hope for Israel and the world. In the womb of the nation of Israel would come the hope of the ages for all men: Jesus Christ. But in Zechariah's day, when he came back to his homeland with the first group of exiles returning to Israel, he speaks of plentiful provision and great joy. Make no mistake. This verse is not about corn liquor or intoxicating wine. It is true corn on the cob and *tiyrowsh*, thirst-quenching grape juice.

Acts 2:13: "Others mocking said, These men are full of new wine."

We should not take seriously the word of mockers who claimed Pentecost included drunkenness from intoxicating wine. The word for wine in this text is not *oinos*, but *gleukos*. One who is not completely devoid of common sense can see in the word a resemblance to something sweet. A person's "glucose" level measures the sugar in the blood.

The people of Pentecost, when the God's Holy Spirit fell, were praising God in *dialektos*, dialects or known tongues, not unknown tongues. The phenomenon, at best, was unrecognizable and unusual. These mockers were jeering and deriding the event. This single mention of *gleukos* in all the New Testament cannot be construed to be intoxicating wine simply because mockery often uses the technique of overkill to defame. Peter defended the truth in the next two verses when he said, "these are not drunken, as ye suppose, seeing it is but the third hour of the day." Peter employs the word *methuo* which is without question the act of drinking to intoxicate. He says these men are not that way. The identifying factor of proof is the time of the day. It was only nine in the morning and according to Peter, who knew the Jewish customs, nobody would be drunk at that time of the morning.

The mockery is false. The claim that *gleukos* was intoxicating is unreliable. F. F. Bruce indicated, "they were filled with new wine – or rather, with sweet wine, for though the vintage of the current year was still some months off, there were ways and means of keeping the wine sweet all the year round."[47]

Revelation 14:10: "The same shall drink of the wine of the wrath of God, which is poured out without mixture into the cup of his indignation; and he shall be tormented with fire and brimstone in the presence of the holy angels, and in the presence of the Lamb."

This is another reference where wine is used in the metaphorical sense as a picture of judgment and wrath from God. It is fermented *oinos* which stifles the senses of the victim. Note that John says this wrath will come "without mixture." The verse with many others proves that Jews mixed their wine. Mixtures were primarily with water, and the standard dilution was four parts water to one part wine. Many times the Jews added spices to their wine to dilute its strength and to improve its taste. But those who have committed spiritual whoredom with the spirit of the age in the end times and worship the Antichrist will drink of undiluted wrath from the throne of God. There is no positive picture of alcohol in this text whatsoever. Why would anyone think that God favors alcoholic wine when He uses it as a portrait of His wrath?

---

[47]F. F. Bruce, *Commentary on the Book of the Acts* (Grand Rapids: Eerdmans Publishing Company, 1984), 65.

Chapter Seventeen

Reviewing the Discovery

An old geezer, who had been a retired farmer for a long time, became very bored and decided to open a medical clinic. Dr. Geezer, we'll call him, put a sign up outside that said: "Get your treatment for $500 - if not cured get back $1,000." Doctor Young, a new, rookie doctor in town, was positive that this old geezer didn't know beans about medicine. He thought this would be a great opportunity to get $1,000 and teach the farmer a lesson. He went to the farmer's clinic, and this is what happened. Dr. Young said to Dr. Geezer, "I have lost all taste in my mouth. Can you please help me?" Dr. Geezer said, "Nurse, please bring medicine from box 22 and put 3 drops in Dr. Young's mouth." With treatment, Dr. Young gasped and said, "Aaagh! This is Gasoline!" Dr. Geezer rejoiced and said, "Congratulations! You've got your taste back. That will be $500." Dr. Young gets annoyed but will not be outdone.

He goes back after a couple of days figuring to recover his money. He comes in to the new clinic and says, "Dr. Geezer, I have lost my memory; I cannot remember anything." Dr. Geezer says, "Nurse, please bring medicine from box 22 and put 3 drops in the patient's mouth." Dr. Young says, "Oh no you don't, that's Gasoline! "Well congratulations," Dr. Geezer exclaims, "You've got your memory back. That will be $500."

Dr. Young, having lost $1000, leaves angrily but comes back after several more days. He says to the fake country doctor, "My eyesight has become weak; I can hardly see!" Dr. Geezer says, "Well, I don't have any medicine for that, so here's your $1000 back." Dr. Young is elated but on his way out the door he discovers he has been shortchanged. Angrily, he looks at the money in hand, looks up at the farmer and says, "But this is only $500." "Congratulations," says Dr. Geezer, "You've got your vision back! That will be $500." The moral of the joke is that it can be costly to forget what you've learned or ignore the cause of your trouble.

What have we learned about the Biblical view of drinking alcoholic beverages? In Chapter One, we discovered that not everything that is called wine in the Bible is fermented, alcoholic beverage. There is no word used for "alcohol" in the languages of the Bible. *Yayin* is a generic term for both fermented and unfermented beverage. *Tiyrowsh*, in nearly every case, is the Old Testament word of choice to speak of unfermented drink coming straight from the grapes off the vine. *Oinos*, like *yayin*, in the New Testament is the primary word for wine, but must be determined by the context of the passage whether it is referring to alcoholic or non-alcoholic beverage. So, it would be terribly wrong to say that when the Bible uses the word "wine" it is speaking of a fermented alcoholic beverage like we have today. If a person will not be honest with what the Bible actually says about wine, then they are guilty and worthy of the indictment of 2 Peter 3:16: "As also in all his epistles, speaking in them of these things; in which are some things hard to be understood, which they that are unlearned and unstable wrest, as they do also the other scriptures, unto their own destruction." It is a dangerous thing to mishandle the Word of God.

In Chapters Two and Three, we discovered that God does not try to cover up sin and the effects of sin in the Sacred Book. Side-by-side with the stories of righteousness are the stories of the destructive behavior of backslidden saints. Noah and Lot sinned with alcohol and reaped horrible life consequences.

Contrast these failures to the two examples of abstinence: the Rechabites and the Nazarites discussed in Chapter Four. The Rechabites were people who by tradition and by righteousness refused to ever bring the first sip of deceiving, alcoholic wine to their lips. The Nazarites took a voluntary vow of holiness that excluded alcoholic wine, even unfermented grapes, from their lifestyle, so they could seek a holy walk with God. Why would God put these two examples in His Book? Obviously, He upholds their behavior, belief and holy living as exemplary consecration for all. But God wanted Jeremiah to see the Rechabites obeyed their human predecessor when Israel would not listen to Almighty God.

In Chapter Five, Solomon, a man who walked away from God in many ways, including drinking alcohol as implied in Proverbs 31:4, becomes the man who gives the sternest warning against alcohol in Proverbs 20 and 23. In Ecclesiastes 2, the king makes his own confession that going after booze as a party animal is "madness of spirit." That comes from the man that the Bible says is the wisest man in all the earth.

In Chapter Six, we discovered that Isaiah, Joel, Daniel, Hosea, Habakkuk, and Moses all join the blessed bandwagon of God that warns against alcohol. Isaiah and Habakkuk tell us there is a curse on it and to leave it alone. Isaiah and Daniel indicate drinking alcohol is associated with idolatry, the worship of false gods such as those worshiped in Babylon which are still known and worshiped today. Hosea warned Israel that alcoholic wine would take their heart away from God. How true that is, even today! Joel tied alcohol consumption to the plague of locusts that cut down their vineyards. Moses warned Israel that Divine destruction was in their future because they had resorted to sacrificing to devils through drunken orgies in Baal worship.

In Chapter Seven, we discovered the sobering reminder that Christians are kings and priests. Since kings and priests were forbidden to drink alcohol in the Old Testament, the Christian is forbidden to drink it today. God is the same yesterday, today and forever. He doesn't change His requirements.

In Chapter Eight, we discovered a truth that bears repeating verbatim: "To associate Christ with the approval of drinking alcohol is Biblically irrational and spiritually insane." Cana was not the scene of a supernatural brewing of alcohol. If Jesus had done that He would have been hypocritically profaning His deity, denying the very purpose for which the miracle was performed in the first place. He also would have been providing 180 gallons of alcoholic wine, an action totally out of character with His Word. Then we also found an eye-opening revelation on how God truly feels about drinking alcohol in Ephesians 5:18. In the inceptive verb, the command "be not drunk" with wine, proves that God is against the process of drinking as well as the state of drunkenness. God hates it when He sees people lift a beer or a glass of wine to their mouth. It is against all holiness and the fullness of the Spirit.

In Chapter Nine, a very important "nail in the coffin" is driven for foolish minds that think "not given to much wine" is a crack in the door for drinking alcohol. To think such is to claim God has a double standard for preachers and deacons. How could God tell pastors they cannot drink alcohol but deacons can drink a little alcohol? The actual counsel, in the wording of the text, is literally do not even hang around it. We learned that if drinking women think it is all right to drink a little, just not "much" wine, this is inconsistent with Titus' call upon their lives to present "behavior that becometh holiness" and be "teachers of good things." Finally, it is unthinkable that "not given to much wine" is permission to drink a little, for in the same logic we would have to accept that Solomon in Ecclesiastes 7:17 was saying we can be a little wicked when we feel like it.

In Chapter Ten, two opposite portraits of wine - one of blessing and one of danger and curse - leaves us with no other option than to conclude that there are two types of wine. There is fermented wine, alcoholic, and there is unfermented wine, the new and fresh squeezed grape juice. This fact simply refutes any claim by the ignorant that all wine in the Bible is alcoholic.

In Chapter Eleven, we gave ample and ancient evidence to prove that the Jews were very capable of preserving grape juice from fermentation for as long as a year. This truth allowed us to debunk the arguments that Jesus had to serve alcoholic wine at the Passover, as stated in Chapter Fifteen. Preservation of the grape juice lasted long after the late fall grape harvest. David Brumbelow, in his excellent book, commented on the Nehemiah 5:18 passage:

> Ancient people were much more knowledgeable and industrious than we give them credit. They knew well how to make numerous variations of drinks. They had numerous varieties of nonalcoholic wine. They had numerous kinds of grapes and other fruit. They knew how to preserve fresh nonalcoholic wine. Contrary to the one-wine theory, Nehemiah had an abundance of all kinds of wine.[48]

---

[48]Brumbelow, 111.

"New wine" is the fresh squeezed juice from the grape. "Must" is the fresh juice of the grape boiled down into a thick consistency, the heat destroying any yeast, thereby preserving the thick liquid from fermentation. This "must" was then diluted with water to make a sweet drink. They called it wine but it was nonalcoholic.

In Chapter Twelve, we proved by the Word of God that there is no distinction made between drunkenness and intoxication. The level of intoxication is not God's measuring stick. God says the fact of intoxication is what He identifies worthy of judgment and damnation. Habitual intoxication, drinking alcohol regularly and socially, indicts the professor of faith in Christ as one who thinks they can mock God. They will be shocked when they stand before God who has the last say. The real believer is described as "such were some of you," no longer desiring to participate in the lifestyles that are named in 1 Corinthians 6:9-10.

In Chapter Thirteen, we discussed three primary motives for abstinence that the Christian cannot ignore. Romans 13:12-14 specifically mentions partying and drinking as a surrender of the Christian identity, and making "provision for the flesh" as well as "walking in darkness." Romans 14:21 calls Christians to refuse to drink alcohol to keep others from being offended and stumbling in their faith, the refusal to do so most certainly causing a loss of influence for Christ. 1 Corinthians 3:17 points out the dire consequences for those who deliberately defile the body, which for Christians is the temple of God's Holy Spirit.

In Chapter Fourteen, a thorough look at 1 Timothy 5:23 proves that the evangelist/pastor Timothy had to take a diluted, minuscule amount of wine to counter a bacterial infection cause by contaminated water. The mere fact that Paul interrupts his discourse of primary instruction to urge Timothy to take the wine, clearly implies that Timothy was a teetotaler. He believed and practice total abstinence. This in no way permits drinking alcohol for recreational purposes or general medication, especially since it has been scientifically proven that grape juice can serve the same medical purpose. Continual use of today's wine for medicine is extremely risky because the wine of Timothy's day was nowhere near the alcoholic content of today's wines. That fact has been proven historically and biblically.

In Chapter Fifteen, it was admonished to never believe the foolish notion that Jesus served alcohol at the Last Supper for two reasons. First, the distinctive identification of the substance in the cup by the phrase "fruit of the vine" prohibits any thought that it was alcoholic. Grape vines do not produce alcohol. Second, alcohol in the cup would have promoted a defiled image of Christ's sacrifice, especially since the leaven in alcoholic wine was considered unholy and to be utterly avoided during the Passover. There was to be no leaven in the bread and no leaven in the cup, no leaven in the house at all.

In Chapter Sixteen we gave a thorough examination of passages that are a bit confusing as to whether God favors drinking alcoholic wine. The very fact that only 26 verses out of 286 are in question suggests great caution before thinking God doesn't favor total abstinence.

If this summary so far is not enough clear evidence of "what the Bible really says about drinking alcohol," then the social, moderate, disobedient, ignorant drinker is judged in his/her denial of the truth. The Bible clearly says to stay away from alcohol.

A man we will call Tommy came to my church regularly for almost a year. He knew my wife who was his counselor. We wanted Tommy to put his faith in Christ and be done with his alcohol. Every time he came to church he was loud and boisterous. His behavior proved Proverbs 20:1 to be true when it says "strong drink is raging." The word "raging" in that passage means loud, clamorous, growling, roaring, or tumultuous. That was Tommy. He didn't have a reverent bone in his body when he was under the influence of the wrong spirits.

Earlier in his life Tommy experienced a serious wreck and had lost a leg. He had been unfaithful to his wife and she had left him. His father-in-law, a preacher, condemned him when he stepped out on his daughter. Yet, Tommy always mentioned that his father-in-law had an affair with another woman in his church.

I shared the Gospel with Tommy as he lay on his couch drinking from a large bottle of Vodka. Tommy began his day with his liquor and ended his day drunk on the floor. He would not accept the cure for his alcoholism even though he would kindly listen to every word about the

Gospel. Tommy always had an excuse. One day I asked him the following question: if he would get up and crouch behind his chair in the living room, would he have to be smaller than the chair to be able to hide behind it? He readily said, "Yes, I would have to be smaller than the chair to hide behind it." I told him that he needed to stop using his father-in-law as an excuse for drinking and refusing Christ because if he hid behind that he was smaller than his excuse. He quickly changed the subject.

I never could lead Tommy to the Lord. His bottle was in the way. If that is not the most tragic pathetic scene, a man going to hell with a booze bottle in his hand, I don't know what is. Tommy came to church for a while but one of the members politely asked him to be quiet while the preacher was preaching. Tommy got up, left and never came back. The church member felt guilty for reprimanding him, but I said, "Tommy was never coming to church for the right reason in the first place." We welcomed him into our church, loved him, but he would not tolerate us or the truth. You cannot play with the liquor bottle and God at the same time.

Chapter Eighteen

How Can I Stop Drinking Alcohol?

Rehabilitation from an alcoholic lifestyle doesn't need a confession, group therapy, or twelve steps. Group therapy, which may help some, often confuses the path of deliverance for the vast majority of people seeking freedom from their addiction. How do I know this? Besides being a pastor, my second job is transporting people to recovery programs every week. My unofficial debriefings with the clients reveal that many consider the rehab programs a joke and just play the game till they get the token, freeing them to resume their lifestyle of choice, which is usually relapse. Others can't find enough truth in the non-faith-based recovery units to lead them out of darkness into the light.

Alcoholics Anonymous purports the doctrine, "once an alcoholic, always an alcoholic." How do I know this? I sat with my son in the program and listened to every word. In the final session, I asked the leader if this system taught that a person is always an alcoholic and cannot ever be free. She responded in the affirmative. This does not square with 1 Corinthians 6:9-11 which says, "Know ye not that the unrighteous shall not inherit the kingdom of God? Be not deceived: neither fornicators, nor idolaters, nor adulterers, nor effeminate, nor abusers of themselves with mankind, nor thieves, nor covetous, nor **DRUNKARDS**, nor revilers, nor extortioners, shall inherit the kingdom of God. And **SUCH WERE SOME** of you: but ye are washed, but ye are sanctified, but ye are justified in the name of the Lord Jesus, and by the Spirit of our God." Jesus can so change a life that the label "alcoholic" becomes past tense. There really is deliverance and freedom from alcoholism if you want it.

Jesus himself promised this deliverance. He said in John 8:32, "And ye shall know the truth, and the truth shall make you free." Then He continued to say in John 8:36, "If the Son therefore shall make you free, ye shall be free indeed." Jesus Christ alone can deliver you from drinking alcohol because He has been given that ministry from God the Father. This is His job, setting people free. In the Temple of Jerusalem, among his critics, He declared in Luke 4:18, "The Spirit of the Lord is upon me, because he hath anointed me to preach the gospel to the poor; he hath sent me to heal the brokenhearted, to **PREACH DELIVERANCE TO THE CAPTIVES**, and recovering of sight to the blind, to **SET AT LIBERTY THEM THAT ARE BRUISED.**" The word "bruised" in that passage means "broken and shattered," which describes many who have come under the cursed effects of alcohol.

If you are reading this book and need that deliverance you can come to Jesus Christ and find healing from the mental, emotional, and physical addiction of alcohol. He will not judge you worthless, but worthy, to receive His forgiveness and freedom from the pull of alcohol or any other addictive substance. You will not find that "free indeed" condition in most rehabilitation or recovery programs. But you will find it in Jesus Christ. However, you must believe the TRUTH to get it. You must believe everything that is shared in this book about what the Scripture declares alcohol to be: a mocker, a deceiver, and a life-destroying sin. God does not in any way, form or fashion favor, condone, or approve the consumption of alcoholic beverages, not recreationally, not socially, not in moderation, not at all. The wine of Bible days was not at all like the wine today. Shun alcohol with all your heart. Come to Jesus Christ, confess your sin of drinking, confess your sinful nature, repent of it for good, and seek God's forgiveness in your life. Through Christ's enablement you can choose to say no to the sins and habits you think you cannot forsake. That is step number one.

Step number two is to change who you run with. 1 Corinthians 15:33 reads, "Be not deceived: evil communications corrupt good manners." The word for "communications" in the Greek is *homilia,* a word that intentionally describes a "companionship." The companions we run with are the ones we communicate with, hang around with, and have support for good or bad behavior. This is why the New American Standard Version of the Bible translates this verse, "Do not be deceived: Bad company corrupts good morals." Even the recovery programs of the world cite this truth as a major factor in avoiding relapse. You can't run with drinkers and expect to stay sober very long. Misery loves company. Jesus said in 15:14 that the "blind will lead the blind and they both will fall into the ditch."

Step number three regards replacing the evil company with righteous company. Jesus taught in Matthew 12:43-45 where a house swept clean but left empty gives a signal to the demonic world that they can move back into the house. Jesus said that seven more demons more wicked than the first one that was run out move in, and the "last state of that man is worse than the first." Alcohol is connected with the demonic world. Any time a person takes leave of their senses, which is what inebriation does to you, this action opens a door for Satan to attack. You need to replace your drinking buddies with genuine believers. You can do that by attending church.

Most alcohol drinkers have decided not to go to church for two reasons. First, they're ashamed. They are not sure if they want to stop drinking or if they can, so they do not consider themselves worthy or fit to go to church. Let everyone know that a sinner in all their filth is the most fit candidate to go to church. Never forget that! I've had alcoholics come to my churches, as I mentioned in the last chapter. Some sit through the message. Some get up and leave because they cannot stand the conviction. I have trained my members to openly receive and love these precious souls who are under attack from the enemy, and believe the lie that alcohol is good for you or able to cover their problems.

Church is where you can find the truth, find good righteous friends, and find an alcohol free lifestyle. Admittedly, there are scoundrels in the Church who have beer in their home refrigerators. Shamefully, there are church folks who drink alcohol in restaurants. Make no mistake about it. God is angry with folks who do that. The Bible says that God is angry with the wicked every day. (See Psalm 7:11) Wicked church members who drink are a disgrace to the Church and to the cause of Christ. They are blinded by the Devil himself, and are guilty of putting a stumbling block in front of sinners. Don't let them lead you back into the ditch. Seek your freedom in Christ. Throw the alcohol away and go to church. Seek out Christ and the true Christ followers so that you can put up a "no vacancy" sign for all passing demons looking at your life and trying to gain entry. For those who are seeking a new way of life, a life of freedom, not bondage, involvement in Church is better than any recovery program.

Three steps, not twelve, is the route to a liberated life. Follow up on these steps by abiding in Christ. That means spending time in prayer to overcome temptation. Spend time in the Bible to learn God's will. Walk with God, not the ungodly. Be filled with God's Holy Spirit by submitting your will to His. In Christ's lifetime here on earth, He recovered the sight to the blind, made the lame to walk again, opened the ears of the deaf, stopped hemorrhaging in a woman who had been plagued with the condition for twelve years, and even raised three people from the dead. Is it unthinkable that this same Jesus could not set a person free from alcohol addiction? Is it impossible for Jesus to change the mind of the stubborn Christian who insists that moderate drinking is acceptable to God? The answer is an overwhelming yes that God can change you if you are addicted or just approve of drinking alcohol. Let your mind be the same as God's. According to Him, wine is "raging" and we are not to even"look upon the wine."

Alcoholism and drug addiction are named the top mental health concerns in Peru by their own psychiatrists. Drinking alcohol begins at an early age, especially for Peruvian males. Though the law states no person under 18 can be sold an alcoholic drink, it is not uncommon to see 10 year olds drinking in the streets with their families or with their peers. They drink a beverage called *chicha*, an inexpensive corn beer which is less than three percent alcohol. Drinking alcohol in Peru is stimulated by the stresses of an impoverished economy, and by cultural norms which brand a person unsocial if you do not drink alcohol with the host.

On one of my first missionary trips to Peru, I stayed in a mountain town called Huaraz. One evening, I was walking back to the missionary compound where we were staying. I noticed a sight that has never left my mind. Climbing the fairly steep hills of that Andean village and puffing for breath because of low oxygen at 10,000 feet elevation, I noticed an animal passing me in the low light of dusk. It was a donkey. As it passed there were leather harnesses connecting the donkey to another passenger, a Peruvian man. The man was drunker than, as we say in the States, "Cootie Brown." He was obviously inebriated, staggering as that donkey was leading him home for the night. The scene was sad but I couldn't help being amused with the grave thought, "which one of the two was the greater ass." Alcohol will reduce a man to poverty, shame, disgrace, and a handicapped life. Don't be that man. It is a dumb life, dumber than a donkey.

Chapter Nineteen

Alcohol and the Devil

From 1920 to 1933 the United States issued a constitutional ban on the production, importation, transportation, and sale of alcoholic beverages. Those days were known by the crusading temperance advocates and the criminal gangsters alike as The Prohibition. A common moniker for the alcoholic beverage at that time was the "devil's brew."[49] Former White Sox baseball player, turned temperance evangelist, Billy Sunday, called it the "devil's rum."[50]

Is there any connection between alcoholic beverages and the Devil? For those who do not believe in a real personal entity called the Devil, there can be no connection. David Nussman cited a report from the Center for Applied Research in the Apostolate (CARA) who dissected raw data from a survey of 1496 adults who professed belief in the existence of God. The analysis stated that 83 percent of Catholics think Satan is just a symbol

---

[49] Linda Emley, "Dry County or Wet? Devil's Brew was a big issue in Prohibition Era," Richmond Daily News Online Edition, August 6, 2018. https://www.richmond-dailynews.com/2013/05/dry-county-or-wet-devils-brew-was-a-big-issue-in-prohibition-era/

[50] Stanton Peele, "The End of the Devil's Brew: Baseball Bans Booze," Psychology Today Online Edition, October 30, 2010. https://www.psychologytoday.com/us/blog/addiction-in-society/201010/the-end-the-devils-brew-baseball-bans-booze-0

of evil, a metaphor for sinful impulses.[51] When large masses of religious people say they believe in God but they don't believe in Satan, there is an apparent glitch in their belief system. Why? Because God himself is the primary witness of Satan as recorded in the Bible.

Jesus Christ believed in Satan. He called him the "father of lies" in John 8:44. The patristic terminology denotes his personhood. In the same verse Jesus referred to Satan as the father of the unbelieving Pharisees. Jesus called Satan a "thief" in John 10:10, who came to "steal, and to kill, and to destroy." Symbols and metaphors cannot do either of the three.

The Bible mentions the name "Satan" 56 times and likewise the names "Devil" and "devils" another 116 times. Both the Old and New Testaments take for granted the existence of a real personal enemy called Satan and his demonic horde of fallen angels (see Isaiah 14:12 and Revelation 12:4). In ages past, Satan led a rebellion amongst the angels of heaven (also called "morning stars" in Job 38:7), and now with fierce resistance seeks to destroy everything that is of God.

Many people refuse to believe in what they cannot see. This is incredibly ignorant and hypocritical. Science can establish the elemental existence of oxygen and none doubt it because humans breathe air everyday in their lungs, which is oxygen they cannot see. They believe in it and require it for survival. Yet, Jesus can tell us about a Devil who seeks to destroy us spiritually, pulling us to hell, and we call that a fairy tale, a superstition of the past from which all men need to be healed. Which one do you think we need to believe in most for our survival: unseen oxygen or the unseen Devil? The answer depends upon your view of life.

Jesus said to Thomas, one of His doubting disciples, "Blessed are they that have not seen, and yet have believed" (John 20:29). Thomas was having some trouble believing Jesus could come back from the dead. He had to touch the body of Jesus to believe. Thomas was a materialist, only

---

[51]David Nussman, "Most US Catholics Don't Believe in Devil," Church Militant Online, August 30, 2017. https://www.churchmilitant.com/news/article/most-us-catholics-dont-believe-in-devil

believing what he could tangibly touch and see. If you are a materialist, you constantly ask yourself, "where is the empirical evidence"? Let me simplify the conundrum for you. Though you cannot see the skunk on the side of the road you travel, you surely know it is near by his unmistakable stench. Satan's work with alcohol leaves behind a horrific stench, though men cannot see him.

C. S. Lewis wrote:

> There are two equal and opposite errors into which our race can fall about the devils. One is to disbelieve in their existence. The other is to believe, and to feel an excessive and unhealthy interest in them. They themselves are equally pleased by both errors, and hail a materialist and a magician with the same delight.[52]

Satan's sinister deception glamorizes liquor, popularizing consumption of wine as the choice of the sophisticated. Yet, the victim never realizes at the front end just how much destruction awaits him. The least blow is the discredit to the Christian's integrity. Worse yet is the naivete of discounting Satan's involvement. There is no enemy so dangerous as the invisible enemy. Refusing to see with eyes of faith the arch enemy of the soul is to fall prey to a multitude of temptations.

For the remainder of this chapter it becomes my worthy duty to make the connection between the seen and the unseen. The very thing that God told us in Proverbs 23:31 not to even look upon begs the question: "Is there a personal, clandestine force driving mankind to drink alcohol"? Through six watchwords in the Bible, I will show you there is a definite connection.

Temptation. James 1:14 says, "But every man is tempted when his is drawn away of his own lust, and enticed." James makes it clear that the man who yields to the temptation of alcohol consumption cannot say, "The Devil made me do it," or "I have a disease, and I have no

---

[52]C. S. Lewis, *The Screwtape Letters* (New York: Harper Collins, 2001) ix.

control over the urges." Granted, long term usage of alcohol increases the addiction factor, but that comes under another watchword to unveil later. The truth, according to God, is that man makes his own choice to take alcohol into his body. James says it is the result of being drawn away and enticed by our own lusts (cravings). But, is it solely coming from within man and no outside force?

The temptation to indulge in alcohol is both internal and external. A. T. Robertson indicated that *exelkomenos* (drawn away) and *deleazomenos* (enticed) are present passive participles.[53] Present passive means the subject is acted upon by an external source. Satan is that source. Man's lust is the internal connection. Like a fish that cannot control the cravings for the worm, man is hooked by Satanic temptation to imbibe the poison.

In nineteen chapters we have thoroughly proven alcohol is forbidden to man by God. At this point, if you insist on drinking alcohol recreationally, socially or habitually you are being drawn away of your own lusts, Satan being the Tempter. More later on that but keep in mind that Satan's hooks and bait would be useless without your cravings.

We not only have to ask what is temptation, but we must reveal the Tempter. Does the Bible really implicate Satan as a tempter? Matthew 4 identifies the external source of temptation. The tax collector Matthew recounted the experience of Jesus as He was "led up of the Spirit into the wilderness to be tempted of the devil" (See Matthew 4:1-11). Therefore, the Bible identifies Satan as the Tempter. However, he would have no success if we, when we are tempted, loved Jesus more than our cravings. I have told many addicts that I, too, have an addiction. They are startled at that admission. Then I tell them that I am addicted to Jesus Christ. He is the One who keeps me victorious over my temptations. Loving Him more than loving what is forbidden, such as alcohol, is the secret to freedom.

How can a man or a woman who drinks find freedom from the constant temptation to drink? Two Bible passages answer this question. First,

---

[53] A. T. Robertson, *Word Pictures in the New Testament*, vol. 6 (Nashville: Broadman Press, 1933) 18.

Hebrews 4:15 says, "For we have not an high priest which cannot be touched with the feeling of our infirmities (weaknesses), but was in all points tempted like as we are, yet without sin." A quick study of Jesus' strategy to defeat the Devil will help avoid alcohol. In Matthew 4, He used Scripture to bolster His resolve. Three separate attacks on Jesus' choices reveals the Tempter's ruthless strategy. God the Son was tempted in the area of **physical cravings** (turning stones into bread after He had fasted 40 days and was voraciously hungry), **prideful confusion** (tempted to doubt God's care, turning attention to personal needs by casting himself off the temple, to see if God would protect), and **personal covetousness** (selling out life's prime purpose by worshiping things instead of God). The draw to alcohol mirrors the exact same temptations. As pointed out previously, Jesus was tempted with alcohol in His most vulnerable condition, the crucifixion, but He refused the temptation (Mark 15:23). It is Christ's power, not yours, that will enable you to say no to alcohol. He is the source for beating temptation. If you have accepted Jesus into your life, then He will gladly help you choose to say no to alcohol. If you are lost, the first step to getting rid of your booze is to accept Jesus!

Second, there is a secret to beating temptation found in 1 Corinthians 10:13. "There hath no temptation taken you but such as is common to man: but God is faithful, who will not suffer you to be tempted above that ye are able; but will with the temptation also make a way of escape, that ye may be able to bear it." The same word that is used in James 1:14 is also used in 1 Corinthians 10:13, the Greek noun *peirasmos*. It is a word which speaks of putting to proof our fidelity in faith and holiness. That is the nature and substance of temptation. Remember that you will never be placed in a proving ground where Jesus has not already been. He can get you through it without yielding to sin.

We do have a way of escape through God's Son. The apostle John shed great light on overcoming temptation in John 14:30. "Hereafter I will not talk much with you: for the prince of this world cometh, and hath nothing in me." Alcohol ceases to be an overwhelming temptation when you realize the formula for victory. If you have everything in Jesus, Satan will have nothing in you. Satan most certainly tempts people to drink alcohol but Jesus overcame him. You can too!

Sober. One of the key teachings of Alcoholic's Anonymous is sobriety. Ironically, for AA, sobriety means abstinence, not just a lack of intoxication.[54] This view leads people to subjectively view their chronic social drinking as harmless because they never consider themselves intoxicated by casual drinking. God says otherwise. Any intoxication is offensive to God and harmful to the Christian testimony. Abstinence is a lack of intoxication for obvious reasons. There is no dichotomy in alcohol consumption according to God.

There is one verse in the Bible which connects sobriety and Satan. The two are juxtaposed in 1 Peter 5:8 as mortal enemies. "Be sober, be vigilant; because your adversary the devil, as a roaring lion, walketh about, seeking whom he may devour." Can a man be intoxicated and free from the Devil's clutches? Is the fact of a woman's intoxication with alcohol putting her in harm's way of the Devil's devouring destruction? The answer to the first question is no. The answer to the second question is yes. I will state the conclusion without doubt: DRINKING ALCOHOL PUTS YOU RIGHT INTO THE GRINDING JAWS OF THE DEVIL. Unless you are sober, in all that the word means, you are a sure target for Satan's deception and destruction.

To draw this firm conclusion I will have to define the word sober. Does it mean to be clear minded, having a calm and collected spirit? Or does it mean to be free from alcohol's intoxicating effects? The exact meaning is crucial for this Biblical passage because it seems sobriety, abstinence from alcohol, effects our vulnerability to Satan. The word "sober" appears in twelve verses in the New Testament. There are two words used in those passages: *sophron* and *nepho*. *Sophron* means to be in one's right mind, exercising self control of human passions. You might understand the word as it is used in present day vernacular when somebody says, "that person has a level head." *Sophron* is a mental function alone. This is not the word used in 1 Peter 5:8.

---

[54]Stanton Peele, "The Meaning of Sobriety," Psychology Today Online Edition, February 17, 2014. https://www.psychologytoday.com/us/blog/addiction-in-society/201402/the-meaning-sobriety

Peter uses the word *nepho* when he speaks of the quality of life which protects us from the Devil. The word is actually the root word for *nephalios* as discussed in Chapter Nine. You recall that this word *nephalios* specifically defined "abstaining" from alcohol. Contrast that with Luke 8:35 where the Gadarene demoniac was "sitting at the feet of Jesus, clothed, and in his right mind" (sophroneo). Peter was not talking about sanity of mind or right thinking. He spoke of deliberate refusal of anything that would dull a man's senses spiritually to the most hungry, fierce, strong, cruel, and greedy pursuer of souls. You had better not rule out alcohol, the world's number one hard drug, as one of Satan's devices to destroy a man (See 2 Corinthians 2:11). When a man drinks alcohol he "gives place" to the Devil to destroy him (See Ephesians 4:27).

Strongholds. Giving place to the Devil may create a stronghold in the believer's life which is hard to abolish. The world calls it addiction, and the Bible, in Hebrews 12:1, calls it a "sin which doth so easily beset us." Paul spoke of these strongholds in 2 Corinthians 10:3-6 when he wrote:

> For though we walk in the flesh, we do not war after the flesh: (For the weapons of our warfare are not carnal, but mighty through God to the pulling down of strong holds;) Casting down imaginations, and every high thing that exalteth itself against the knowledge of God, and bringing into captivity every thought to the obedience of Christ; And having in a readiness to revenge all disobedience, when your obedience is fulfilled.

Neil Anderson called them "fortresses" and said, "Strongholds are fleshly thought patterns that were programmed into your mind when you learned to live your life independently of God."[55] The "programmer" is Satan. His access to the computer of our minds comes by our lost condition before saved (See Ephesians 2:2), and by surrendered territory after we're saved (See Ephesians 4:27).

---

[55]Neil T. Anderson, *The Bondage Breaker* (Eugene: Harvest House Publishers, 2000) 60.

Before we are saved (a total surrender of our life to Jesus Christ), we "walked according to the course of this world, according to the prince of the power of the air." (Ephesians 2:2) Paul drove home the point that an unbeliever has no control of his walk. He has no power over his fleshly urges. The unbeliever cannot quit alcohol without Jesus Christ living on the throne of his heart. The unbeliever is called the "child of disobedience." He cannot walk away from the beer can or the wine bottle until he decides to turn in the direction of Jesus, our Saviour. All of his life is a "stronghold" of Satan.

The child of God, a child of obedience, has a resident power within Him, the indwelling power of the Holy Spirit, to turn away from habitual sins. According to Ephesians 4:30, after we're instructed to give no place to the devil (verse 27), these habitual sins, which have become guarded fortresses of Satan, grieve the Holy Spirit. Now picture this reality. At salvation the Holy Spirit becomes the eternal resident in a man's heart. The Holy Spirit is the third Person of the Godhead. That means He is God and is just as Holy, thrice Holy, as the Bible says of God the Father (See Isaiah 6:3, Revelation 4:8 and Habakkuk 1:13). He is the Spirit by which we are sealed unto the day of redemption. He lives inside you, if you're a child of God, and you're pouring alcohol in on top of His head and His residence? How deeply do you think that grieves Him? How inconsistent is that with your stated personal faith? Are you not ashamed to the depths of your soul for this conduct?

Satan loves it. He loves the very exhale of hell's heat from your lungs as you state, "there's nothing wrong with drinking alcohol as long as you don't get drunk." You've lied against the Word of God. He loves to see the shining, demon-water on your lips as you liquor-talk the loveliness of your sin. Satan says, "I've created a stronghold, a fortress, from which I have control. She gave it to me. He gave it to me. It's mine and I can beat this sucker around as long as I want to if I can just keep him drinking. He won't be able to think right. He won't be able to have close fellowship with God. He is my victim by a bottle."

Strongholds are hard to tear down. They are not built in a day and they'll not be torn from their footers in a night. Repentance can be immediate. Forgiveness can be swift and permanent. But removal of a stronghold may take years to rip apart and reverse. That being said, they can be torn down. It starts and continues in the "imaginations." The word "carnal" means seated in the human, depraved, natural nature of man rather than seated in the Holy Spirit. Substance abuse victims are carnally deceived by psychological concepts purported to deliver them from the jaws of hell's lion. But hear it carefully. Psychology won't work. Group therapy, as I've seen it, only spreads the affliction by the sharing of carnal ideas, a further travesty trying to find a cure. Transference, Replacement Therapy, set a date, keep a diary: this is the jargon of the false physicians. Our weapons are not carnal. They're spiritual. They "cast down" imaginations that exalt themselves against God, and bring into obedience every God-defying thought.

You cannot know what IS of God until you know what IS NOT of God. Our mighty weapon against strongholds is the Bible. It is the Word of God. It is a powerful weapon according to Hebrews 4:12. Use it! Satan is no match for the Word of God.

When my family moved to "the farm" in 1963, we had no indoor bathroom. We had an outhouse. My mother threatened that she would not move from town to the country farmhouse till dad built her a real bathroom on to the house. She conceded her hesitancy to move with the firm promise from dad that he would give her the city comforts soon. However, he delayed too long. Several weeks went by and my mother impatiently took a whole day using a crow bar and a hammer to tear down that little outhouse to force the issue. She was hot, sweaty, filthy dirty when dad walked in from work that evening and said, "Joyce, what have you been doing today that you've gotten so dirty?" He hadn't even noticed that the outhouse was gone. Mother explained what she had done. Then my dad added insult to injury when he said, "Why Joyce, you didn't have to work so hard; I was going to take the tractor, tie a rope around it, and just pull it down." My mother was furious. Dad got the bathroom built, with my uncle's help, in two weeks.

That story illustrates for me the fact that strongholds need a suitable weapon for their demolition. They don't fall with crow-bar and hammer work. They need the bulldozer or tractor work of God's Word. They also need the dynamite of prayer. Powerful things can happen through prayer and prayer partners. Strongholds must have the fresh winds of the Spirit of God uprooting every inch of their foundation. Play not, my friend, with the carnal weapons - the deceptive toys of the Devil's Deceiving Deliverance Programs. Grab hold of the Word of God, and fill your life with it if you want to see real deliverance. Jesus can do it (John 8:36).

Flesh. The triple whammy for the Christian is the world, the flesh and the devil. Consider 1 John 2:15-17:

> Love not the world, neither the things that are in the world. If any man love the world, the love of the Father is not in him. For all that is in the world, the lust of the flesh, and the lust of the eyes, and the pride of life, is not of the Father, but is of the world. And the world passeth away, and the lust thereof: but he that doeth the will of God abideth for ever.

Oh, you didn't see the devil in there? Wait, and momentarily I'll show you where he is hiding.

Alcohol is of the world, that is, of the world system. It is a product that has created great division between the righteous and the wicked. The world system is the system that exalts man over God, material possessions over eternal passions, and fleshly desires over righteous living. How is that system connected to Satan? The Devil is not only the "prince of the power of the air," but he is also the one who perverts everything that is Godly. John said there were three things in the world that are "not of the Father." If they are not of the Father, they are of Satan. These are the lust of the flesh, the lust of the eyes, and the pride of life. Satan inspires all three.

Satan not only works through the world system to deceive us. He works through the flesh to tempt us. The apostle Paul wrote in Romans 7:18, "For I know that in me (that is, in my flesh,) dwelleth no good thing: for to will is present with me; but how to perform that which is good I find not." Combine this verse with James 1:14, and we readily see that lusts (cravings) originate in the flesh.

The regenerate man (one who has been truly converted to faith in Christ for salvation) has a dual nature. He is both flesh and spirit. Paul expressed the war that goes on inside man's being, even the best Christians, which overcomes us often in the heat of temptation. Alcoholics drive by a liquor store, and a fight ensues in their mind as whether or not to turn around and buy the booze that so entices their flesh. Backslidden Christians are invited to a wedding where wine and beer are served, and their flesh cries out to be "one of the crowd" celebrating the moment. Satan enjoys every moment of the battle that rages within us. He wants us defeated. He loves the surrender to sin.

How do we defeat the flesh? Make no mistake about it. The battle is fierce with three enemies against us: Satan, the world, and the flesh. Even Jesus Christ sought to alert his sleeping disciples about the difficulties of the battle in Matthew 26:41, "Watch and pray, that ye enter not into temptation: the spirit indeed is willing, but the flesh is weak." If you want to know where the battle between the spirit and the flesh is won, simply read Romans 7:24-25. "O wretched man that I am! who shall deliver me from the body of this death? I thank God through Jesus Christ our Lord. So then with the mind I myself serve the law of God; but with the flesh the law of sin."

While in the body, the warfare between the flesh and spirit will carry on the constant, perilous combat against temptation. We will not escape that battle till the spirit and soul of man is released from the body in death. Until then, freedom from alcohol temptation or any other temptation is found in Jesus Christ when our mind "serves the law of God." Frankly, the battle against alcohol is won in the Word of God. If you or I ever expect to be victorious over the lust of the flesh, the lust of the eyes, and the pride of life, our best strategy is found in the little verse learned early in children's Sunday School, "Thy word have I hid in mine heart, that I might not sin against thee" (Psalm 119:11). Speak the Word. Trust the Word. Obey the Word. Fight the battle using the Word. Watch the Word work in your life. Stay connected to Jesus.

Pergamos. Located 15 miles inland from the Aegean Sea, Pergamos was considered Asia's greatest city. By the time John wrote the Revelation, Pergamos had been Asia's capital for almost 250 years. There is no record in Acts of the establishment of a church in Pergamos, but John's record obviously indicates a missionary presence sometime on Paul's second missionary journey (see Acts 19:10). Pergamos survives today as the Turkish city of Bergama. The name Pergamos means "parchment," pointing to the great library of parchments located in this city. Hippocrates studied in the library at Pergamos.

Not only was Pergamos a great city of learning, it also served as an important center of worship. MacArthur commented:

> Pergamum was an important center of worship for four of the main deities of the Greco-roman world, and temples dedicated to Athena, Asklepios, Dionysos, and Zeus were located there. But overshadowing the worship of all those deities was Pergamum's devotion to the cult of emperor worship. Pergamum built the first temple devoted to emperor worship in Asia (29 B.C.), in honor of Emperor Augustus.[56]

These identifications explain why the apostle John wrote to the church at Pergamos in Revelation 2:13 saying they dwelt "where Satan's seat is."

In addition to the discussion on worship of Dionysius and Bacchus in Chapter Six (See MacArthur footnote on "Bacchanalian feasts"), I want to call your attention to the worship of the false god, Asklepios, in Pergamos. MacArthur reiterated the aggravated idolatry that made it Satan's throne:

> When you went to the temple of Asklepios you went there to be healed. In the temple harmless snakes slithered all over the temple floor. And in order to be healed you had to go in there and lie down and stay there. You slept on the temple floor and while you slept the defused multiplicity of the deity of Asklepios crawled over your body and infused you with his healing power. Satanic? Yes.[57]

---

[56]John MacArthur, *MacArthur New Testament Commentary: Revelation 1-11* (Chicago: Moody Publishers, 1999) 85.

[57]John MacArthur, "Pergamos: The Church at Satan's Throne," https://www.gty.org/library/sermons-library/66-8/pergamos-the-church-at-satans-throne

The rod of Asklepios is the symbol of medicine, a single coiled snake around a rod. The field of medicine today has accepted the corrupted symbol, the "caduceus," two serpents intertwined around a pole with wings on top. The modern symbol has nothing to do with medicine and is actually attributed to another false god, Hermes or Mercury. Yet, both symbols have snakes. This pagan symbol dates all the way back to the fourth century B.C.[58] Physicians prescribe drugs. The Bible word for sorcery is *pharmakeia*. Does that sound familiar? Is there any connection between drugs and the city where Satan's throne sits?

James Way commented on the manipulative treatment in the temple of Asklepios:

> There they used every means of healing imaginable. They used both medicine and psychology–and about everything else. You go down long tunnels, and above are holes that look like air holes for ventilation but are not. As you walk along these tunnels, sexy voices come down through the holes, saying to you, "You are going to get well. You are going to feel better. You are going to be healed." You go down to the hot baths where you are given a massage. There is a little theater there where they give plays of healing. If they haven't healed you by now, as a last resort they put you in that temple at night and turn loose the nonpoisonous snakes which crawl over you (That is known as the shock treatment in our day). If they don't heal you, they will drive you crazy, that's for sure. They have a back door where they take out the dead. They don't mention the ones they don't heal; they speak only of those who recover. Caesar Augustus loved to go there. He wasn't exactly sick; just an alcoholic. They just dried him out every year. May I say to you, healing was satanic in those days. There is no question about the fact that there were good men there who used medicine, but basically, it was satanic.[59]

---

[58]See https://en.wikipedia.org/wiki/Rod_of_Asclepius

[59]James A. Way, *Mounting Rareness: Characteristics of Growing Christians* (Bloomington, AuthorHouse, 2011), 26.

It is safe to assume that if they used hypnotizing female voices and slithering snakes, and dogs to lick open wounds, onsite medicine for altered states of consciousness would be included in the protocol of this establishment. We know that Asklepios used divination (witchcraft), incantations, and homemade liquid medicine to cure diseases.[60] He was an alchemist, just like the infamous, drugged, false prophet Nostradamus.

The most telling claim about this false Greek god is an anecdote from his childhood. Asklepios aided a snake, and the snake returned the favor by licking his ears clean and teaching him secret knowledge about medicine.[61] This is why the priests of the Asklepion (healing temple dedicated to the god Asklepios) depended on dreams and visions given to their patients while they slept in the temples overnight to concoct a medicine for their afflictions. Those who have their "senses exercised to discern both good and evil" (Hebrews 5:14) understand the blessing of good medicine, but they have to ask a most pertinent question about the Asklepios cult. Who is the god behind the gods of Greek mythology and divination inspired medicine? It is none other than Satan!

Whether you believe it is speculation to assign drug usage to an ancient cult in Pergamos, the fact remains that alcohol consumption alters the mind and the body. When that happens you have put both mind and body up for grabs by Satan. Paul established this truth when he wrote, "In whom the god of this world hath blinded the minds of them which believe not, lest the light of the glorious gospel of Christ, who is the image of God, should shine unto them" (2 Corinthians 4:4). The "god of this world" is Satan, and his favorite target is man's mind. Introduce alcohol in that world system and you have a sinister god afoot that makes Asklepios look like a choir boy. Alcohol doesn't open up the door to a problem-free life. It opens the door to the Tormentor, the Devil.

Cup. There are two cups in 1 Corinthians 10:21. "Ye cannot drink

---

[60] See http://www.theoi.com/Ouranios/Asklepios.html

[61] See https://eclecticlight.co/2016/10/24/the-story-in-paintings-aesculapius-or-asclepius/

the cup of the Lord, and the cup of devils: ye cannot be partakers of the Lord's table, and of the table of devils." The cup of the Lord and the cup of devils do not go together. If the "cup of devils" included alcohol, there is no clearer warning from God than this passage that a Christian cannot drink, must not drink alcohol. To understand what the cup of the Lord and the cup of devils refers to, you have to examine the Corinthian context.

The Corinthians had asked Paul if it was all right to eat meat that had been offered to idols. Corinth was saturated with temples of idol worship. They had the Temple of Aphrodite where more than a thousand temple prostitutes offered their bodies to worshipers based upon the erroneous belief that their union increased the fertility of the land. The very name "Corinth" became a synonym for immorality.[62] They had the Temple of Poseidon, ruler of the sea and maker of earthquakes, whom everybody feared and worshiped for the preservation of their city. There was the Temple of Apollo, the god who harnessed his chariot daily to four horses and dragged the Sun across the sky.[63] With twelve temples to false gods, Corinth was a seed bed of wicked idolatry. Paul was concerned that the Christians in Corinth would be infected by the scourge of idolatry and forsake their faith in Christ. This concern gave rise to his adamant command, "Wherefore, my dearly beloved, flee from idolatry" (1 Corinthians 10:14).

The apostle then began to address how this idolatry crept into the church at Corinth. Communion with God and communion with devils cannot happen in the life of a Christian. This explains the word "flee." Have no part with idolatry. The stage of the apostle's argument was the Lord's Supper. When Jesus instituted the Lord's Supper, on that fateful night before His death, He said something that Paul repeated to the Corinthians. Jesus said, "And he took the cup, and gave thanks, and gave it to them, saying, Drink ye all of it; For this is my blood of the new testament, which is shed for many for the remission of sins" (Matthew 26:27-28).

---

[62]See https://www.padfield.com/2005/corinth.html

[63]See http://apologeticspress.org/apPubPage.aspx?pub=2&issue=785&article=2338

Paul said, "The cup of blessing which we bless, is it not the communion of the blood of Christ?" (1 Corinthians 10:16) What is the meaning of this word "communion"? That is the key. If you understand that you will understand the adamant command to flee idolatry.

The word for "communion" is the word *koinonia*. Jesus said to remember him every time we take the cup and the bread. But it is more than remembrance. Koinonia means sharing, fellowshipping, participating, partaking, communion. Let me illustrate it for you. We refer to the cup and the bread as symbols. Compare that with a picture of your deceased loved. Is the picture only a symbol? No. Every time you view that picture you enter into an intense connection with the portrait. Memories flood your mind as if the person is still with you. That is how Paul pictures communion with Jesus in the Lord's Supper. Christ becomes so real to your spirit. You enter into the "fellowship of His sufferings" (Philippians 3:10). You are actually having fellowship and participation in your mind, as well as your heart, with the great sacrifice Christ paid to forgive your sins. In the same way, the Corinthians needed to know that they could not go to these temples of idolatry because such action put them in communion with devils. They were making a connection.

Does drinking alcohol put you in communion with devils? It sure does. How so? Anything you are not willing to forsake, when God has called you to forsake it, becomes an idol. An idol is nothing according to 1 Corinthians 8:4, but the demons connected to the idols are real. Since Satan is the prince of this world, he is the power influencing the world system. When Christians give in to the flesh, and drink alcohol, they have drunk from two cups that are fiercely in contention with one another. Never will a Christian so violate the sanctity of the Lord's Supper than when they follow the cup of the Lord with a cup of alcohol. Not only is it inconsistent with the testimony of Christ, it is a sacrilege against Christ.

The following story came to me from one of my dearest friends, Dr. Kevin Shearer, missionary in Peru for over 20 years. I am relating the story to you verbatim.

> We hosted a team from two churches—one from Knoxville, TN; the other from Oklahoma City. Their purpose in coming was evangelism through medicine. Our setup was unique, in that we

set up triage, medical, optical, and dental stations to meet the many needs in the area we chose to work. The final two stations were pharmacy, followed by spiritual medicine.

In one particular church, the New Life Baptist Church (where I took Bro. Tim to do some prayer walking in 2018), spiritual medicine was in the main auditorium. We had moved all furniture out and set up small stools to sit on and speak with people. I had about 6 American volunteers, plus translators in the room. One man staggered in off the street, instead of coming through the established system. We sat him down with one volunteer, a young man from Memphis, who was also fluent in Spanish. I was busy with other patients but checked on the young man from time to time. He insisted he could help the man, who was progressively louder.

After more than 30 minutes, the young college student deferred to me. I turned my stool to face the man and asked him if he wanted to be free from the chains that bound him. He began to whine and share the same story we had all listened to for the past several minutes. I told him firmly to stop talking and look at me. He stopped talking and tried to look at me. His bloodshot eyes were turning in opposite directions, he appeared to be so drunk. I asked him again if he wanted to be free. He said, "Yes, but they won't let me." "Who?" I asked. The man said fearfully, "The spirits." "What spirits?" I asked. "The spirits of alcohol," he groaned.

Then his eyes opened wide with fear and he cried, "Here they come now!" With that, this man went stiff and fell backwards onto the ground. The college student wanted to grab him and help him up. I told him not to touch the catatonic man. I began to rebuke the demons of alcohol that appeared to have such a grip on him. After several minutes, the man roused and sat up. His eyes were clear; there was not one sign of drunkenness. He smiled and said, "I am free. I am really free!" I told him he was not yet free and presented to him the gospel of the Lord Jesus Christ. The man prayed earnestly, with a passion that we seldom see, and began hugging everyone in the room and anyone who would come near him, thanking everyone for helping him find freedom in Jesus.

You had better believe it. Alcohol and the Devil are connected. They are connected through temptation, the command for sobriety (abstinence), through the pull of the flesh, through strongholds, through communion with devils, and through idolatry.

I would like to tell you another story of temptation to alcohol. Two young teenagers were good friends by multiple connections. They lived in the same community. They rode the same bus to school. They went to the same church. Their dads worked as engineers at the same company. The company picnic was always scheduled for late fall. This particular year the picnic was being held at one of the boy's farm. There was an excitement in the air. Good food, games, hay rides, and homemade ice cream were just a few of the thrills anticipated.

There was a drink machine set up by the local Coca Cola company. It was the pull type where the soft drinks poured out of a mechanical spout. The two young men were assigned to operate the drink machine and they were fascinated about the task. One by one the employees came by the drink stand and the boys delighted in filling their cups.

Somewhere in the early morning hours of the picnic the two boys discovered that a part of their task was opening the top of the drink machine where the beer was stored in ice, and handing those who requested it a "cold one." Neither boy cared for that task because both were raised with Christian values. Their convictions were that beverage alcohol was wrong. One of the boy's dad said that if he had known the company was going to bring beer he would not have let them use the farm for the occasion.

Late that afternoon temptation struck. One boy asked his friend, "have you ever tried beer; would you like to try it together; which one have you heard is good"? Neither boy had ever tasted beer. They both popped the top of a popular brand and sipped. Immediately, one of the boys spit the nasty tasting brew out. The other boy took three sips and quit. The boy who spit out the devil's brew was myself. The other boy was my friend, Chuck Pritchard. We laughed together but I am so glad Satan never hooked me or Chuck on this life-destroying, testimony-ruining liquid.

Chapter Twenty

Wishing For An Alcohol-Free World

I, for one, if I were the only one, would be proud and elated if planet Earth would outlaw all alcoholic beverages. I cannot think of one, in the whole lineup of booze bottles, that would be necessary for man except perhaps a sterilization agent for a wound on a remote battlefield. I would be tickled to never ever see again a box truck, van, or semi-truck with the logo Budweiser on the side. Something turns sour in my stomach and spirit when I see that. I think of all the lives this hellish liquid has destroyed. I would be so thankful if I could go to any restaurant in America and never see Christians I know, or strangers, sipping their mixed drinks and wine, destroying their testimony for Christ with every sip.

I would rejoice to see citizens of this land, where you can read "In God We Trust" on their public buildings and on their coinage, lining the freeways and back roads of our God-blessed nation in massive unity pouring out on the road every bottle of liquor, beer and wine. Let the peddlers surrender their wares, let the citizens pour it all out on the ground, and let the makers of air fresheners donate to the cause of covering up the stench.

Is there anything so heart-sickening as fetal alcohol syndrome where babies are born with shrunken heads; deformities of the eyes, nose, and lips; central nervous system abnormalities; lifetime social skill deficiencies; and motor skill impairments, to name a few? Mothers, stop drinking alcohol. You're hating your baby when you do that. Innocent ones have their life wrecked by careless, self-centered mothers.

Finally, it is time to be done with the grief at the hospitals, the cover-up at the funeral homes, and the secret abuse in the living rooms of America. When alcohol has become a god, and we had rather continue cleaning up the mess rather than arresting the real culprit, America has a conscience problem. It is a $58 billion industry.[64] Alcohol related deaths claim 88,000 lives annually in America.[65] Nearly half of the 78,000 liver disease deaths are caused by alcohol consumption.[66] Who is going to stem the tide of this killing spree by one culprit? I'm under no delusions that one book will solve the vast problem with alcohol, but I want to be found in the fight against this ever prevailing evil.

My deepest desire is that many Christians will read this material and find a rallying point in their spirit to raise up truth that has "fallen in the streets." I have mentioned the writing of this book throughout the days of its composition to many people, and you should have seen the frowns I got. Silence captured the moment of the mention. I just smiled back. We should not be ashamed of old-fashioned Christian convictions based on Biblical truth no matter how many people try to frown it down. Smile back and defend the truth. Jude 1:3 is a rallying point for the fight. "Beloved, when I gave all diligence to write unto you of the common salvation, it was needful for me to write unto you, and exhort you that ye should earnestly contend for the faith which was once delivered unto the saints." The word "contend" means to agonize for those faith convictions found in the Word of God. There is more power with truth than there is with a lie.

May the Christian who is compromised with the truth be so smitten within the pages of this apologetic work. I hope the backslidden saints

---

[64]See https://www.ibisworld.com/industry-trends/market-research-reports/retail-trade/food-beverage-stores/beer-wine-liquor-stores.html

[65]See https://www.livescience.com/46547-alcohol-linked-premature-deaths.html

[66]See https://www.ibtimes.com/us-alcohol-abuse-deaths-binge-drinking-all-rise-2635179

who are given to occasions of alcohol consumption will see themselves crucifying the Son of God afresh and putting him to an open shame (Hebrews 6:6).

We should preserve the testimony of Jesus through our lives at all costs. I know Baptists who absolutely ignore the old Church Covenant that used to hang on the walls of their churches. As I wrote this, I went to three Baptist websites, inspected their Church Covenant, and was shocked to discover they had removed the "alcohol clause." The original covenant was urged voluntarily on Southern Baptists, and the alcohol clause read, "to abstain from the sale and use of intoxicating drinks as a beverage." Parents and grandparents would turn over in their grave if they could see their children and grandchildren imbibing what they were taught to refuse.

How I wish that some unsaved person would pick up this book and read Chapter Eighteen on how to come to Jesus and be delivered from the cursed alcohol. Yet, alcohol consumption is just one of a multitude of mankind's sins. All of mankind must realize that we are sinners, by birth (Psalm 51:5), by nature (Jeremiah 17:9), and by choice and practice (Romans 7:15-25). Sinfulness in our lives causes death: not only physical death, but also spiritual death (separation from God in everlasting torment in hell). In light of this soul-shaking truth, the good news is so wonderful. Romans 5:1,6 says, "Therefore being justified by faith, we have peace with God through our Lord Jesus Christ: For when we were yet without strength, in due time Christ died for the ungodly." Let man know that it is not so much sins (plural) that need God's forgiveness but sin (singular), the sinful nature, the bent towards choosing sin, that needs the loving grace of God. This is the Gospel that changes a man's heart. If you can understand this simple truth, and can receive it, there is only one more step to take. "Whosoever shall call upon the name of the Lord shall be saved" (Romans 10:13). Ask God to forgive you of all your sins, your sin nature. Turn your life over to Christ. Decide to turn in the opposite direction of sin. Serve Jesus Christ with your life and lips.

Finally, let the mommas be at peace because their sons and daughters have chosen abstinence. Let the drunkards find freedom from the booze in Christ's delivering power. Let the highways be safe by a radical repentance from alcohol. Let the school children lift their heads in pride when they think of their moms and dads who never bring wine and beer into their homes. Let the preachers continue to bring the fire of God's holiness against alcohol consumption, pressing with all of Heaven's appeal to eradicate it from our planet. Let the children of God "soberly" watch for the Lord to return. I am going to a world without alcohol and the very thought of heaven delights my soul.

I can think of no greater way to conclude than giving you a poem shared by one of America's prince of preachers, R. G. Lee.

Jack and Jill

Went up the hill,

To get some bootleg liquor;

Jack went blind

And lost his mind -

And Jill is even sicker!

(Unknown, *quoted by R. G. Lee*)

Bibliography

Books

Anderson, Neil T. *The Bondage Breaker*. Eugene: Harvest House Publishers, 2000.

Bruce, F. F. *Commentary on the Book of the Acts*. Grand Rapids: Eerdmans Publishing Company, 1984.

Brumbelow, David. *Ancient Wine and the Bible: The Case for Abstinence*. Carrollton: Free Church Press, 2011.

Davis, J. D. *Davis Dictionary of the Bible*. Grand Rapids: Baker Book House, 1924.

Gaebelein, Arno C. Gaebelein's Concise Commentary on the Whole Bible. Neptune: Loizeaux Brothers, 1985.

Gately, Iain. *Drink: A Cultural History of Alcohol.* New York: Gotham Books, 2009.

Jaeggli, Randy. *Christians and Alcohol: A Scriptural Case for Abstinence*. Greenville: Bob Jones University Press, 2014.

Lewis, C. S. *The Screwtape Letters.* New York: Harper Collins, 2001.

MacArthur, John. *MacArthur New Testament Commentary: Revelation 1-11.* Chicago: Moody Publishers, 1999.

Masters, Peter. *Should Christians Drink: The Biblical Case for Abstinence*. London: Sword and Trowel, 1992.

Morris, Henry M. *The Genesis Record*. Grand Rapids: Baker Book House, 1976.

Patton, William. *Bible Wines or the Laws of Fermentation and Wines of the Ancients.* New York: National Temperance Society and Publication House, 1874.

Rice, John R. *The Best of Billy Sunday.* Murfreesboro: Sword of the Lord Publishers, 1965.

Robertson, A. T. *Word Pictures in the New Testament.* Vol. 6. Nashville: Broadman Press, 1933.

Merrill F. Unger, *Unger's Bible Dictionary.* Chicago: Moody Press, 1957.

Vine, W. E. *Expository Dictionary of Old and New Testament Words.* Old Tappan: Fleming H. Revell, 1981.

Way, James A. *Mounting Rareness: Characteristics of Growing Christians.* Bloomington, AuthorHouse, 2011.

Wiersbe, Warren W. *Be Alive.* Wheaton: Scripture Press Publications, 1986.

Internet Sources

AFP/Relaxnews, "One Drink A Day Can Increase Cancer Risk"https://www.newsmax.com/health/health-news/alcohol-drink-daily-cancer/2018/04/25/id/856518/.

Bryner, Michelle."How Much Alcohol Is In My Drink?" https://www.livescience.com/32735-how-much-alcohol-is-in-my-drink.html.

Emley, Linda."Dry County or Wet? Devil's Brew was a big issue in Prohibition Era," Richmond Daily News Online Edition. August 6, 2018. https://www.richmond-dailynews.com/2013/05/dry-county-or-wet-devils-brew-was-a-big-issue-in-prohibition-era/

Kaiser, Walter C. "Jesus In the Old Testament," *Gordon Conwell Theological Seminary Online*. http://www.gordonconwell.edu/resources/Jesus-in-the-Old-Testament.cfm)

MacArthur, John. "The Divine Pattern for Relationships," https://www.gty.org/library/sermons-library/90-97/the-divine-pattern-for-relationships.

MacArthur, John. "Pergamos: The Church at Satan's Throne," https://www.gty.org/library/sermons-library/66-8/pergamos-the-church-at-satans-throne

Nussman, David. "Most US Catholics Don't Believe in Devil," *Church Militant Online*. August 30, 2017. https://www.churchmilitant.com/news/article/most-us-catholics-don't-believe-in-devil

Peele, Stanton. "The End of the Devil's Brew: Baseball Bans Booze," *Psychology Today Online Edition*. October 30, 2010. https://www.psychologytoday.com/us/blog/addiction-in-society/201010/the-end-the-devils-brew-baseball-bans-booze-0

Peele, Stanton. "The Meaning of Sobriety," *Psychology Today Online Edition*, February 17, 2014. https://www.psychologytoday.com/us/blog/addiction-in-society/201402/the-meaning-sobriety

Serrels, Nathalie. "Alcohol is an Acquired Taste," *Recovery Navigation*. https://recoverynavigation.com/alcohol-is-an-acquired-taste-so-why-do-we-bother/#.W2HIV1uPLIU

Shifferd, Scott J. "What Kind of Wine Did Jesus Drink?" https://godsbreath.net/2011/05/20/did-jesus-drink-wine/

Smith, Dr. William. "Wine," *Smith's Bible Dictionary*. 1901, https://www.biblestudytools.com/dictionaries/smiths-bible-dictionary/wine.html.

Tee, Buddy."Rare Gene Discourages Alcoholism Among Jews," *Very Well Mind*. https://www.verywellmind.com/rare-gene-discourages-alcoholism-among-jews-63179.

Vine, W. E."Wine," *StudyLight*. https://www.studylight.org/dictionaries/vot/w/wine.html.

Wikipedia, "Temperance Movement,"https://en.wikipedia.org/wiki/Temperance_movement.

Wikipedia, "John Edgar," https://en.wikipedia.org/wiki/John_Edgar_(minister).

Wikipedia. "Independent Order of Rechabites," https://en.wikipedia.org/wiki/Independent_Order_of_Rechabites.

Magazine Articles

Stein, Robert "Wine Drinking in New Testament Times." *Christianity Today*, June 20, 1975, 9-11.

Made in the USA
Monee, IL
24 June 2021